Ceaseless Explorer
Conversations with Joseph Spies

Michelle Rogge

The University of South Dakota Press
1995

Ceaseless Explorer
Conversations with Joseph Spies
by
Michelle Rogge

Copyright© 1995
The University of South Dakota Press

All rights reserved

Library of Congress Cataloging-in-Publication Data

Spies, Joseph R.
Ceaseless explorer : conversations with Joseph Spies / Michelle Rogge.
p. cm.
Includes bibliographical references.
ISBN 0-929925-29-7
1. Spies, Joseph R. 2. Chemists--United States--Biography. 3. Photographers--United States--Biography. I. Rogge, Michelle, 1961- . II Title.
QD22.S63A3 1995
540' .92--dc20
[B]   95-10734
                                 CIP

Cover design
Patricia Peterson

Cover Photograph
Dr. Joseph Spies

Editor
Patricia Peterson

Published at Vermillion, SD
April 1995

On Catalina Island, 1928

At the time of his retirement

Dr. Joseph R. Spies

Acknowledgments

Expressing my gratitude to the people who helped me with this project is difficult—I have so many people to thank!

First, I must thank Carl Spies and his wife Karen for being so flexible and generous with their time during my stay in Washington, D.C. They cheerfully chaufered me from place to place and even gave me a tour of famous sites.

Second, I must thank Pat Peterson from USD Press for having faith in my abilities and giving me the opportunity to write this book. She has worked with me patiently, draft by draft, offering invaluable suggestions and insights which have worked their way into this book. Without her this book would not be what it is.

Third, I extend my profound thanks to Dr. Joseph R. Spies for being such a great subject to interview... for having led such an extraordinary life.

Last, but certainly not least, I want to thank my son Benjamin for understanding when Mommy went to Washington, D.C. without him.

MR
March 1995

Preface

One evening, my wife Marj and I were having dinner with Pat Peterson, managing editor of USD Press, at a local eating establishment known more for its treatment of tenderloin steak than its ambience. When the steaks had disappeared, I began telling Pat some of the adventures of an older friend of mine, Dr. Joseph Spies. After only a few stories, Pat looked me firmly in the eyes and said with some intensity, "This man's life must be shared with others." I could not have agreed more.

Dr. Spies is a 1927 alumnus of the University of South Dakota with a B.A. in Chemistry. I first became acquainted with him in 1987. He was visiting the University because of his endowment of a scholarship program for undergraduate chemistry majors. During his stay he was making a formal presentation of a bound volume of his scientific papers to the Chemistry Club. It was my role to escort him to the second floor of the building in which he once studied. He started the climb of the long flight of stairs at my own brisk pace, but, knowing the gentleman was 86 years old, I expected to slow to his pace quickly. I could only look on with some amazement as we neared the top of the stairs and he showed no sign of slowing or exertion. As I was soon to discover, physical vigor was not the only amazing thing about this man.

My professional and personal admiration for Dr. Spies grew as I became better acquainted with him and his work. The volume of his publications is the public record of an outstanding scientist of great dedication. One of his publications is one of the most cited papers in the chemical literature. However, it is not his record of accomplishment in chemistry that has had the greatest impact on me.

During his career as a chemist, he began photographing animals, particularly cats and birds, and he became an animal rights advocate. While he enjoyed some early successes in photography, Dr. Spies did not turn to photography in earnest until his retirement. Then he attacked this new period in his life with the same energy and dedication he had brought to the challenges of his South Dakota childhood, the rigors of his professional career, and the tragedy of his wife's struggle with Alzheimer's disease.

It appears there was no place he would not attempt to go to take pictures of animals, nor was there any technical photographic problem he wouldn't tackle. Australia, Patagonia, the arctic circle (which he visited when he was 87 years old), the South Dakota Badlands, the zoo, his own backyard—his creative energies took him to all of these places. He designed and built equipment to improve his photographs.

My own appreciation for the quality of his photographic work began when Dr. Spies visited the University a second time. He had increased his scholarship endowment and was also presenting a second bound volume, this one a record of his photography career, to the Chemistry Department. He also brought along several gallery-sized, framed pictures for a public showing of his work. As Dr. Spies and I were taking the pictures down after the exhibit, I rather timidly suggested that it would be nice to have one of his pieces for permanent display. Then everyone could see that his creativity was not restricted to chemistry.

He looked at me with some startlement and said, "Why didn't I think of that before?" With his easy generosity, he asked me which one I would like. I already had one in mind. Because of my own youthful experiences, I have a special attachment to squirrels. I also have a fondness for blue jays, perhaps as much for their deviltry as for their beauty. "As long as I am asking," I responded, "I will ask for the best," and I indicated his photograph of a blue jay sitting on the edge of a bowl of peanuts with a peanut in its mouth. The blue jay is obviously startled by a squirrel, which had just climbed a post and thrust its head up over the other side of the bowl. The photograph was one of his favorites, too.

The picture is special to me, not only because of its beauty and its resonance with my own personal experiences, but because it is a symbol for me of a very special person whom I will remember with great fondness even when I reach Dr. Spies' age, if that is my privilege. Dr. Spies has become a role model for me, especially as my own retirement is now less than a decade distant. Few others are better examples of the creative use of that time of greater personal freedom.

With his body finally telling him not to stray too far from home, I have wondered how this man, who has led such an intense and active life, would respond to this very different kind of challenge. Part of the answer is provided by this book. When I first raised the possibility of it with him and told him of the impact I believed it would have, he was chagrined. As the author of several books, he realized he was no longer able to do it alone. It was no small thing for this independent man to say, "Yes, but you will need to help me."

The request led to a partnership in writing this book between two very different individuals—the older, conservative, traditionalist, scientist-artist and a young, definitely nonscientist, liberal, unconventional writer. The combination worked beautifully. The sensitive reader will note the impact Dr. Spies has had on this book's young author.

I welcome the reader to the delightful experience of getting to know Dr. Spies. His accomplishments and character encourage and warm the hearts of those who have known him personally. As you read this book, you will join the circle of his friends.

Howard Coker
March 1995

Ceaseless Explorer
Conversations with Joseph Spies

> We shall not cease from exploration
> And the end of all our exploring
> Will be to arrive where we started
> And know the place for the first time.
>
> —*Four Quartets*
> T.S. Eliot

Introduction

Meeting Joseph Spies was surely an experience of changing perceptions. At no point during the interview process was I able to classify him neatly as either a chemist or a photographer— a South Dakotan or an Easterner — an animal rights advocate or a scientist who believed in using animals for research.

The facts: he was born in South Dakota, the son of immigrant parents. He spent three years in a South Dakota orphanage. He earned an undergraduate degree in chemistry in the 1920s at the University of South Dakota. After a brief interlude of working his way to California and herding sheep, he earned a Ph.D. in chemistry and spent most of his life in Washington, D.C. working for the U.S. Department of Agriculture. He published more than eighty academic papers in his field.

Somehow during this time, he slipped into photography, first as a hobby and later as an effort that resulted in the publication of five books about cats and other animals. Then, in his late seventies and early eighties, when most people would be tucking a blanket around their knees and taking afternoon naps, he travelled to the Arctic, Australia, Patagonia and other exotic places in the world.

I read all of this and a great deal more in preparation for my meeting with him at his home in Arlington, Virginia. But the research did not prepare me for what I would actually find when I arrived at Dr. Spies' home.

2

I had been told of Dr. Spies's heart condition beforehand and that he had to take it easy these days, so I expected to meet a tiny, frail old gentleman — he was nearly ninety after all — confined to an easy chair. Instead, I was confronted at the front door by a tall, clear-eyed, sturdy man, who looked twenty years younger than his actual age. Right away I suspected this man didn't have a clue what it meant to "take it easy."

Dr. Spies showed me around his house. In almost every room I was greeted by striking photographs of cats and other animals, mounted on the walls, leaning up against chairs, placed in huge piles. He told me about some of them briefly. As he talked, I began to sense that he was a shy man; in order to get over initially awkward moments with strangers, he talked about what he knew best. I was surprised to observe that the author of two cat books—who at one time had owned 13 cats—now had none. Dr. Spies seemed astonished that I even noticed.

"I haven't had any cats in years," he said. Obviously, as much as Dr. Spies loves cats, this was a part of his life he had put behind him.

Dr. Spies, his son Carl, Carl's wife Karen, and I had coffee in the dining room before Dr. Spies and I set to work. We shared some light conversation, but I soon discovered that Dr. Spies had his mind focused on the task ahead — telling his life story to me for the next several days. He sat in his chair, drumming his fingers on the armrest, obviously waiting for the pleasantries to be over. He had spent weeks preparing for my visit and was more than ready to begin.

At one point, Carl teased his father, saying, "Dad, I don't think I've seen this table cleared off like this in years." Every house, I've observed, boasts a room that is its heart, where everyone congregates, where people eat and talk and feel most comfortable. Clearly, the dining room, with a TV in one corner and two easy chairs in opposite corners, with the telephone nearby, and the cleared-off dining room table in the center, was the heart of Dr. Spies' house. Some of his favorite animal photographs were mounted on the walls, and, as crowded as the dining room was, there was an air of constant use and hominess that the other rooms lacked. Those other rooms, with their relatively neat but neglected piles of photographs, books, and papers, seemed to represent completed segments of Dr. Spies' life on which he had closed the doors. It was obvious that the dining room was where Dr. Spies lived now.

After Carl and Karen left, Dr. Spies and I sat down at the dining room table to begin the interviewing process. Late afternoon sunshine poured through the front windows and the kitchen window that faced us.

Dr. Spies brought out several pages of notes—many of them typed, since, as he explained, "I have trouble with my handwriting." He waited, observing intently how I set up the tape recorder and tested it to make sure it was working properly. Ever the scientist, Dr. Spies obviously had prepared to conduct a carefully controlled experiment, but now he seemed concerned that I might be the one variable he would not be able to control.

Before he began reading from his notes, he carefully instructed me as to how we should proceed, saying, "I would like you to engage me in conversation at any time so we can flesh out things and stimulate some thoughts I hadn't had before."

I did as he requested, at one point asking him, "Dr. Spies, do you have any regrets?"

Spies paused. He had been reading steadily from his notes, and I had interrupted his train of thought. He set his notes on the table and looked at me. "In the last twenty years of my life, I've had more time to reflect on what I did, and there are a number of things that I'm very ashamed that I did—but I'm not going to tell you what they are."

We both laughed at his answer. But that was my challenge in interviewing Spies, that provided the tension to our conversations—getting him to reveal not so much his "dark" secrets (as he feared), but what made Joseph Spies tick, what drove him to accomplish so much. Dr. Spies' "experiment" — telling the story of his life — got out of control at times, which was necessary for it to succeed.

With that, the least I can do is to start where Dr. Spies wanted me to begin.

1

Early Years on the Farm

As soon as I turned on the tape recorder, Dr. Spies began his narrative, reading steadily from his notes.

"I was born in Madison, South Dakota on November 5, 1904, but I don't remember living there. My family moved to a farm two miles northwest of Madison, and that is where my first consciousness occurred.

"I loved the farm. In the spring when the snow melted, I was fascinated by the rivulets of water, the farm animals grazing in the pastures, the growing things, both animal and plant.

"We stayed on the farm mostly. We rarely went to town, except to buy grocery items we couldn't grow on the farm ourselves. I learned to ride a horse bareback when I was only five or six. Once"—here, Spies smiled as he read—"the horse slipped down into a hole and fell, but, luckily, neither the horse nor I were hurt. That was one of my earliest narrow escapes.

"My father, Joseph Michael Spies, had married my mother, Helen Dhalberg, in Sioux City, Iowa on March 8, 1893. My mother didn't do farm work, but she collected eggs from the chickens, gardened, ran the house, and took care of us. My parents were both immigrants, and while my father never spoke

Joseph Michael Spies and Helen Dahlberg

German around us, my mother would fly into Swedish with her relatives whenever they visited."

I asked, "Did you ever visit Germany or Sweden?"

Spies shook his head. "No, I have no desire to do that. I stayed in this hemisphere from top to bottom." He laughed to himself.

I had the feeling from his statement, "I have no desire to do that," that if he did have the desire to go to Europe now, he would do just that—regardless of his age or heart condition.

Spies continued, "Arthur, the oldest child, was the only one born in Sioux City; the rest of us were born in Madison, South Dakota. All together my parents had ten children, five of whom lived to adulthood —Arthur, Helen, Earl, myself, and the youngest, Ruth. Five children died as infants. That was common." Spies looked up from his notes and smiled. "Isn't it amazing that out of all that mess I should be here?"

"Yes, it is," I commented. "You were tough."

Spies chuckled. "I must have been. I remember my mother was kind and patient when I was very young. I had a great fear of dying. Somewhere I had heard that if my heart stopped beating, I would die. I needed to ask my mother to listen to my heart on many occasions. She might have had her hands in dough or been busy cooking things, but she would patiently stop what she was doing and put one hand over my heart to make sure it was beating."

"Why do you think she did that?"

"Because I was afraid." He said this as if I should know it. "I thought my heart could stop any time and that I would die."

"What made you think this?"

Spies shrugged his shoulders. "I don't know. Why does a child think anything?" And he laughed at his own question.

Later, it occurred to me that, even though he didn't say so, he might have been afraid because he had seen infant brothers and sisters die. Life was obviously much more precarious in those days.

Spies continued with his narrative. "One winter I had a severe cold or something like influenza or pneumonia. I'm not sure what it was, but I remember being very sick.

"The upstairs of our house was not heated. There were just registers on the first level, where the heat came through the floor from the downstairs heaters. My mother sat up all night with me downstairs where I could stay warm, and she looked after me. Under her loving and attentive care, I got well quickly."

I asked, "How big was your school? Was the classroom regular size or more like a country school?"

"Oh no. I attended the normal school in Madison," he explained. "It's a practice teachers' school. It was in town, a nice school, although not very efficient"—he chuckled—"as you'll see later."

I smiled, charmed by Joseph Spies' wry sense of humor. I hadn't counted on a doctor of chemistry being able to appreciate what was funny about his own life.

Spies continued, consulting his notes once more. "It was about two miles to school. In the wintertime I sometimes rode in the buggy. One time when I had to walk, I froze my ears. When they finally thawed out, they were wrinkled, with water dripping out of them, which is pretty serious, but I didn't realize that at the time."

"I take it you weren't wearing earmuffs."

He laughed. "They didn't fit very well if I was. The next morning I heard the older children saying that it had been forty degrees below zero that night. You can imagine what it was like to go to the bathroom with the outdoor plumbing, when the temperature was less than forty below—especially if the wind was blowing." He laughed again. "That was really a problem."

Unexpectedly, Spies paused, looking directly at me. It was obvious from the hesitation in his eyes that something had occurred to him that wasn't in his notes, that he wasn't sure how to explain, or even if he wanted to explain it. "My father—I told you he was a German—and he was kind of a hard man in some ways. I hate to tell you this story. I had a dog that I loved very much. Unfortunately, it started chasing the pigs. One day my father shot the dog.

"He didn't tell me he shot him. He said he shot up in the air and the bullet came down and hit the dog, which I believed at the time. The dog died in my arms. It was only years later that I found out he actually shot the dog because it was chasing the pigs."

I wasn't sure how to respond to this obviously painful childhood memory. I only commented, "He was trying to spare your feelings a bit, it sounds like."

Spies nodded, almost with relief it seemed to me. "He was, yes. He only gave me one spanking—which I probably deserved." He laughed, although uncomfortably this time. "I don't remember what the cause of it was. He didn't have too much to say to me."

Obviously, he was bothered by talking about this. I decided to change the subject. "Did you and your family go to church?"

"My mother was a Baptist, but I'm not sure about my father," he said. "I did become a Baptist and go to church with my mother. My father didn't go very often."

"Can you remember any times where you and your brothers and sisters did things together? Fun things?"

"Oh, Ruth and I were companions, sort of. We used to go outside and play with the farm animals. One time we were playing, pretending that we were stalks of grass. And the horses were eating along, and they'd push us out of the way. But this time, one of the horses stepped on Ruth's foot—and he was so tame, he wouldn't get off right away." Spies laughed heartily. "He stayed on her foot until he was good and ready to get off it."

"She must have been screaming in pain," I observed.

Spies looked sheepish for a moment, as if he were ashamed at having laughed about a horse stepping on his sister's foot. "Well, she was. Oh, I used to get up on the roof of the hog house and tie an ear of corn to string—twine—and then throw it out to the hogs. When they'd come to get it, I'd jerk it away from them." He laughed again.

I was surprised to hear this from a self-proclaimed animal lover. "Oh, so you were tormenting the hogs!"

Spies laughed. "That was really funny."

He continued, "One night—it must have been in the summer—Ruth and I decided we were going to stay out all night together, sleep outdoors during the night. We sneaked out that night, fully intending to sleep outside in a nearby wagon under the big sky until morning. But when the lights went out in the house and things got real dark, we got scared and went in the house." He smiled. This was clearly a happy memory for him.

We took a break from the interview process at that point. Dr. Spies was tired, and we had accomplished a lot in an hour and a half. I had expected to spend this afternoon getting acquainted—but, amazingly, we had forged ahead with the interview, delving into some vivid and occasionally painful childhood memories.

I listened to the first tape that night, mulling over some of what he'd said. I couldn't help but wonder how this South Dakota farm boy ended up as a retired chemist/photographer in Washington, D.C. I was eager to know more.

When I arrived the next day, Spies picked up where he left off. This idyllic life on the farm—as he described it—would come to an abrupt halt on April 20, 1913, when he was only eight years old. In the hard times that followed, he would remember those early years on the farm with a great longing.

Irene Ruth Spies and Joseph R. Spies
at about three and six years old.

2

Life in the Orphanage

"One chilly spring day," Spies recalled, "I was playing outside. Relatives were visiting, and my mother was sick in bed.

"Then my aunt came outside to tell me that Mother was dead. She had been ill with pneumonia, but I never understood how ill until that moment. She was only forty-four years old.

"It was a sad and frightening time, adjusting to life without my mother, but eventually I did. Life continued on as before. I lived with my father and the rest of my family the following year on the farm.

"In 1914 my father put the two youngest children, my sister Ruth and me, in the orphan home in Dell Rapids, South Dakota, which was maintained by the Independent Order of Odd Fellows at Dell Rapids, South Dakota. I think I would have resisted it terribly—leaving the farm—but I don't remember a thing about it. It must have been so traumatic that I just put it out of my mind."

I asked, "Why did your father send you away?"

Spies said, "He just felt like he couldn't take it. There were five of us children, living."

"You were nine years old?" I probed. "How old were your brothers and sisters at the time?"

Spies said, "My younger sister Ruth was six. We were the two that were sent to the home. The others were older. The only thing I remember about it...I don't remember anything about leaving or the trip down there or anything, but I do remember that night after everyone had gone home. I heard my sister crying in her bed, in the night."

Dr. Spies was quiet for a moment; his hands trembled slightly. He struggled to hold back tears. I sensed that he had not talked much about this experience, and I was quiet too, waiting for him to regain his composure.

He cleared his throat and continued. "The first year at the home was not very pleasant. We had a matron named Miss Miller who ran the home like a tyrant.

"I was hungry most of the time. The amount of food we received had no relation to our appetites. One time I was so hungry that I parched corn on the furnace shovel to eat, and I even sucked a raw egg that I found outdoors. We also wound up periodically being given a dose of Epsom Salts for constipation. It's the worst tasting stuff in the world. I can't —" he laughed— "it was terrible. They would line up the kids every so often, and we'd go in the bathroom and be forced to drink this stuff."

I asked, "Was there a big problem with constipation?"

"No, no, there wasn't," he said, shaking his head. "It was just— what do you call it—a part of the procedure— a prophylactic treatment, I guess." He chuckled. "So we didn't get any trouble. We were also put into a room for fumigation."

"Why was that?" I asked. "Was there a problem with ...lice?"

"No, no. It was ...a prophylactic." Spies laughed again. "They would use a cloth dripping with formaldehyde to fumigate us. We had to stand in this room, crying, and, of course, tearing. I wasn't frightened, but we sure didn't like it. It was very uncomfortable."

I tried to picture this scene. "Did they fumigate all of the children at once?"

Joseph Spies at I.O.O.F. Home,
Dell Rapids, SD

"I remember a room full," he answered slowly. "They must have had us do it in groups, you know. I don't know exactly how long we were in there—maybe half an hour or so."

I imagined groups of children standing in the fumigation room, huddled together, not completely understanding what was happening to them.

"That must have seemed like an eternity," I said.

Spies laughed. "Yes, it did. I also was kept out of school one day for an entire day to scrub the long hall on hands and knees, as a form of punishment. I don't remember what my crime was, but I worked from morning until afternoon to complete the job.

"Not everything during this first year was bad. We were allowed to go exploring in the countryside, which included the Big Sioux River and the Dells, a beautiful quartz formation. I was also given permission to trap muskrats in the fall." Dr. Spies looked up at me almost apologetically. "At that time, I was still part of traditional South Dakota in respect to trapping and hunting. My brother used to hunt jack rabbits at home. It was a staple item of our food, especially during the wintertime."

"So you just mainly trapped muskrat?"

Spies answered, "Yeah, and skunks and so forth, for the skins. I would skin them myself. And I would sell them, too—just made a few dollars from it. I tended my traps before school, walking through a cemetery in the darkness of very early morning. It was the shortest route to take, but it was quite eerie walking by myself among the tombstones. My young mind easily conjured up ghosts and other frightening creatures. It really used to be very scary to walk through that cemetery in the dark. I had to do this in the morning before school and get back.

"In the winter, the other kids and I had terrific snow battles. Sledding and bobsledding on the hills in the winter was great.

"I had a couple of roommates, two boys who shared a room with me at night. I used to tell them stories about going to the moon and other things like that. They loved to listen."

Surprised, I asked, "You made up these stories?"

Spies nodded. "Yes. I didn't realize they would come true in my lifetime."

"Were you unique among the children at the Home, as far as having a parent? Were the rest of the children orphans?"

Spies said, "They varied. At that time they had old folks living in the Home, too, people at the end of their lives—just like a nursing home. And the children ranged from—well, they didn't have any babies in there. The children were able to take care of themselves, although there were some little tots in there. There were no babies, though."

That didn't exactly answer my question, but I decided not to push it. From talking with others, I learned later it was common in those days when the mother died for the father to place children in other people's care—family or otherwise.

Spies continued. "At the end of the first year, there was an investigation at the Home. We got a new matron, Grace Sutphin. She was kind and ran the home with love. My sister Ruth, who stayed in the Home for eight years, told me that she felt a real affection for Grace who became her companion. Grace even took her on trips."

I asked, "There was quite a difference between her and Miss Miller?"

Spies nodded. "I think there must have been some kind of scandal, but we were just children—we didn't know anything about that. There was an investigation, and Miss Miller was fired—I don't remember her first name. I had only been there for a year when she got fired.

"In spite of the problems at the I.O.O.F. Home, the people running it did their best to instill good values in the children. We were raised to tell the truth at all times. We were taught honesty." He looked at me earnestly. "I don't want to give the wrong impression. I told you about that first terrible year. It wasn't like that all the time. It really was a good place, in many ways."

I asked, "What was a typical day like in the Home? When you would get up, what would you do first?"

Spies said, "We'd clean up and have breakfast in a long room where we all ate together. And the matron sat at the head and"—he laughed—"parceled out food."

"Was it decent food, after the one woman left?"

"Yes, it wasn't so bad even when she was there," he answered, smiling.

"What would you do after breakfast?"

"On weekdays, we would go to school," he said. "We were encouraged to do well in school. We were given good literature to read. We had *The Youth's Companion*, a biweekly or monthly magazine. It's long out of print. I also remember reading *The American Boy.*"

I asked, "What was *The American Boy?*"

"Oh, it was a little more elaborate than *The Youth's Companion,*" Spies said. "It came monthly, I think. Very good reading for kids. I also read animal stories by Thornton W. Burgess, who had a tremendous impact on my thinking about animals. This eventually led to my becoming an animals rights advocate—completely the opposite of the way I started out, hunting and trapping."

"What stands out in your memory about Burgess' animal stories?"

Spies said, "His main thesis that I remember was that... he taught me... Grace Sutphin gave me one of his books for Christmas, *Tommy and the Wishing Stone.* It was my favorite Burgess book. The main character, Tommy, would go somewhere out in the country and sit on this magical wishing stone. And he would wish that he could be a certain animal, and then he would turn into that animal. And then he would have a story about that animal and what he did and all that. That's how I came to appreciate animals had feelings too. There were several animals in the book. There were about a dozen stories or so. Oh yes, and I loved the illustrations—Harrison Cady did them—they were fantastic."

I asked him what else he remembered about his schooling.

Spies paused. "Oh yes—I attended Madison Normal School for the first four years, from grades one through four, including the year after the death of my mother in 1913. When I was enrolled at the Dell Rapids Public School in the fifth grade, the shock of changing schools was great. I flunked every subject I took the first semester. I really worked as hard as I could, but I just couldn't get it. It was beyond me. I cried."

Changing schools seemed to me to be the least of young Joseph Spies' problems. Losing his mother and being sent to an orphanage would explain his difficulties in adjusting to a new school.

Spies continued. "Mary McCullain, who was my teacher, made me repeat every course. She flunked me in everything. Strangely enough, in later years, I really wanted to go to this person and thank her for what she'd done. She was the turning point in my life."

Astonished, I asked, "Weren't you traumatized by this?"

"I suppose so," he said, "but I got what I deserved."

Many educators today would disagree with this viewpoint, but I kept my thoughts to myself. "What finally turned you around?"

Spies said, "I don't know. I just finally caught on. Of course, Miss McCullain was more helpful to me than she might have been otherwise. After I repeated this semester, I received a Bronze Liberty Bell, which is an award for being the best student. And she's the cause of that. I owe Miss McCullain a great debt of gratitude for treating me as she did because I was always near the top of my class from then on." Spies smiled with pride.

He continued, "That first semester, I also became the target of a town bully.

"The students at the Home walked to school, the little kids in front—about four abreast— with progressively taller students bringing up the rear. I, being younger, walked toward the front.

"The bully was a town student who didn't live at the Home. For some unknown reason, he singled me out. Every day he would come up from behind me and get a scissor-hold on me. Do you know what that is?"

Spies showed me what a scissor-hold looks like. I winced.

Spies continued, "He would wrap his legs around me and lock them until I was squeezed like a vise. I thought I was going to die—the pain was unbearable."

"How old was he?" I asked.

"Oh, he was practically a man," Spies answered. "He was much older than I was. I couldn't resist him at all. He was much larger than me.

"The other kids from the Home did nothing to help me. I suppose they were afraid he'd do the same thing to them. Finally,

I told the authorities at school about it. He stopped torturing me, although he would occasionally make remarks and give me dirty looks." He laughed, adding, "I could live with that."

"What about girls? Did you have anything to do with girls at that age?"

Spies said, "As a matter of fact, I do remember a girl at school sent me a valentine during my last year there. I remember to this day how thrilled I was. I did have a certain tender feeling toward her, but I never got the chance to talk with her. Getting that valentine was one of the highlights of my life."

"Did you visit the family farm while you were in the Home?"

"No, I didn't," he said, shaking his head. "And my father never visited. As a matter of fact, the only family member who visited Ruth and me was my brother Earl. He used to write us letters too. He felt terrible about our being placed in the orphanage, although he never said anything about it at the time. Many years later, shortly before his death, he confessed to me that it still bothered him."

Although I didn't speak up at that point, it bothered me too. I couldn't imagine how hard that would be on a small child and how much resentment I might harbor toward my father, how abandoned I would feel.

Spies read my mind. He said, "What is surprising to some people is that I never had any bad feelings against my father for putting my sister and me in the Home. I always felt that he was doing what he had to do, what he thought was best for us at the time. I never had a single feeling towards him all of my life because of that—I mean, bad feeling."

I found the way he said that interesting—"I never had a single feeling towards him all of my life because of that."

I asked, "Did he write letters to you?"

"No," he responded. "As I said, Earl did."

"How long did you stay at the home?"

Spies said, "For over two and a half years. Then, in 1917, I went to my brother Arthur's home, to live on the farm where I had spent my early years. My father had moved off of the farm and my brother Arthur had moved on to it."

"Did your father retire then?"

"No," he explained, "he took another job, working for Standard Oil Company of Indiana. I guess he felt he wasn't making enough money farming to keep doing it."

I asked, "Were you relieved to leave the home, or did you have mixed feelings?"

"No, I was glad to leave the home."

That answered my question, but I wasn't satisfied. "When you left there, did you think about how you were different after that experience? It must have been a very emotional experience coming back to the farm."

Spies said, "Well, I don't remember any emotional feeling about it. Years later, I came back to Dell Rapids to the Home and gave a talk on a cats. They had a reunion of people who had

Spies in "Sunday Best" on farm.

lived there. There were many people who were so bitter they wouldn't come back. Now, I never felt that way. I had no bitterness toward the people at the Home. As a matter of fact, I always used to say, no matter how hard you have to work physically, if it doesn't impair your health, if you can get through it, it will strengthen your character."

I commented, "Evidently, those people didn't think their characters were strengthened."

Spies laughed. "Oh, I can see why they might have felt bitter, if they were there at the same time as I was and went through the first year with that matron. That would make some people bitter. However, they probably just dwelled on it and dwelled on it, which destroys a person inside. I never thought anything about it."

He added, "I received my traditions at the Home. Such great training. We learned about honesty, hard work, religious beliefs, so much that has floated by the liberals of this country. I learned a person should work at a profession they love."

I found it surprising that Spies didn't feel any bitterness about those hard years in the home and was, in fact, grateful for what he had learned there. But what surprised me even more was that Spies didn't bear his father any ill will for placing him in that home. What's more, he was proud of the fact that he felt no resentment toward him.

Later, I talked with others who provided me with some insights into what things must have been like in rural South Dakota in the pre-WWI years. Finally, I understood.

In those days, children did not criticize their parents or even "talk back to them." They were taught to respect their elders and not question the decisions they made, good or bad. People from that era usually don't resent their parents for what they might have suffered as children.

However Spies looked at his experience—positively or negatively—I couldn't help feeling that those three years in the I.O.O.F. Home had changed Spies forever.

3

Back on the Farm

Spies went on, "I continued with my education at Madison Normal School, skipping a semester. My education at Dell Rapids, as I realized later, had been superior to what Madison could offer me at the practice teacher's school. I finished eighth grade at Madison without any problems, riding horseback to school every day.

"At that time I also hunted and trapped, although my ideas were changing. Everybody was against gophers then because they would eat the corn that the farmers planted. So people would trap and shoot gophers. One time I freed an animal that was caught in such a trap."

I glanced through my notes. "You mentioned the author whose books you always read as a child—Thornton W. Burgess. Was he part of what started to change you over?"

"Absolutely," Spies answered.

"When do you think were the critical years when you went from a hunting and trapping mindset to the other side?"

Spies looked intently at me. "I've thought about this many times. One time a couple of snowy owls came down and I took a shot at them."

"How old were you?"

"I'm not sure. I hadn't been under the influence of Thornton Burgess for very long. But I think how terrible that was to do."

He was being pretty hard on himself, I thought. I asked, "At the time, did it bother you, or not?"

"Well, it sort of did," Spies answered. "But it didn't bother me enough so that I didn't do it." He sighed. "It took a number of years before I completely got it out of my system to be a hunter and a trapper."

"You must have been starting high school about this time."

He nodded. "I entered the Madison High School in the fall of 1918. Then, they closed the school down for about three months because of the Great Influenza Epidemic of 1918. People were dying likes flies. I spent most of the time husking corn for my brother Arthur. Then I had the misfortune to catch a cold. I was put in an isolation house with flu patients."

I observed, "That was pretty risky to put you in there, with just a cold."

"I know. They just slapped me right in there and put me in a bed alongside the flu patients, some of whom were dying. It's a wonder I didn't catch the flu from them. Apparently, I didn't."

"This was 1918—how old were you then?"

Spies said, "I was fourteen."

"You must have been very aware of World War I then. Did you think the war was going to continue at that point, or did you think about it at all?"

Spies shrugged his shoulders. "I didn't think about it too much. When the United States got involved, my brother Earl volunteered. As a matter of fact, he was in France for seventeen days under fire. Fortunately, he came out of it all right. I never thought of Earl being killed, you know. It's just like...I wouldn't think of myself being killed, although I could have been, if I'd had to fight. When they announced the war was over, I remember the bells were ringing in all the towns. A great celebration."

I asked, "What happened then after you got out of the isolation house?"

"I returned to the farm then, going to school once it resumed and working for my brother Arthur." He smiled. "I remember riding about two o'clock in the morning when—Ebba was her name—Arthur's wife was to have a child. And I remember I had to ride on horseback to town to get the doctor, and I heard her screams and stuff when she was having...she had the baby down on the farm, you know. They had three, altogether. I used to babysit them."

I tried not to laugh. I couldn't quite picture Dr. Spies babysitting three small children.

He continued. "I think it was in my sophomore year of high school that my father sent me to live in Madison with a family of a widow lady with four children; her name was Mrs. Hilde. I used to play shinny, which is hockey, all day Saturdays. They had an ice rink near a school."

"You called it what? Shinny?"

"Yes, shinny," Spies answered. "I guess it's because you get hit in the shins a lot."

The Spies farm house.

We both laughed. I asked, "Who were your biggest influences in high school?"

Spies said thoughtfully, "No one stands out. The football coach, Lowry—I think he taught physics. And I enjoyed him very much."

"What were your strengths—could you already see what your areas of interest were—in high school? Did you tend to go toward the sciences more than other areas?"

Spies nodded. "Well, yes, I guess I did like the science courses."

"Can you remember what sort of things you liked to read at that time?"

"I read a number of novels—Civil War novels—*My Lady of the North* and *My Lady of the South*. There was a whole bunch of stories like that, that I read. I was a voracious reader during my high school days. But from then on, I didn't read very much—I didn't have time."

Spies' choice of reading material surprised me. I imagined him reading non-fiction works on science or even history. But novels? I never would have guessed that.

Spies continued. "In my junior or senior year of high school, I bought a pony, a mare, which I kept at my brother Arthur's farm. When I went to work for Frank Graf, another farmer, I kept my horse at his place. He had a stallion that he took around to the nearby farms for breeding purposes, you know. While my mare was at the Graf farm, she got pregnant. Frank never told me that his stallion had anything to do with it, but I imagine he did."

"So your horse gave birth."

"Yes," he said. "Eventually, I sold the colt to Frank."

"Maybe he had it planned," I commented, smiling.

Spies laughed. "I think he did."

I asked, "When did you graduate?"

"I finished high school, leaving there in 1922. I just missed a scholarship by one person being ahead of me—my best friend, Harold Moon. As it turned out, he didn't use the money from the scholarship." Spies shook his head over this missed opportunity.

"Then I received an offer of $25 a month to herd sheep on a nearby farm, from a man named Rath. This seemed like a million dollars to me, and I was sorely tempted to do it. However, my sister Helen encouraged me to go to college instead. Helen was all for all the education you could get. She thought that college was the touchstone to greater things, although she really didn't know any more than I did. She was just a little bit older, by four years.

"At the time, I couldn't see the importance of getting a college education. Twenty-five dollars a month looked awfully big to me. Fortunately, I decided to take Helen's advice, thinking she might know something I didn't."

"It sounds as though your sister had quite an influence on you."

Spies said, "She did. She knew all the social graces, unlike myself."

"How do you suppose she acquired the social graces?"

"She stayed with Mrs. Hilde and her family and engaged in social activities to a greater extent than I."

"By social graces, do you meaning dancing, for example?"

Spies nodded. "That was one thing."

"Tell me," I said, "do you think those years in the orphanage, without your mother or the rest of your family, had something to do with your lack of social graces?"

Spies paused. "This is something that's been on my mind. One of the things that I missed most in my life, because I didn't have anyone to advise me on certain matters, was that I didn't develop any social graces. I had no one to give me any advice on how to act. Oh, I acted all right because I was sincere and honest, but I was crude. I wasn't polished. I had no way of knowing what you were supposed to do in certain social situations."

I asked, "How did you become aware of this?"

"Well," he chuckled, "I wasn't, at first. Afterward, always afterward, I would see the error of my ways."

"Did anyone else in your family give you guidance besides Helen?"

Spies said, "Oh yes. My brother Earl was an extremely ambitious, hard-working man. He was the more responsible of the two brothers, actually." Spies laughed. "It's rather interesting that, during the 1920s, when he was farming, he went broke. He didn't declare bankruptcy or anything. He paid all of his debts. Later, he had a business in Coleman, South Dakota. Coleman's about fifteen to twenty miles east of Madison. He got rich off it, making his money selling oil."

I commented, "That's so funny to think of some little town in South Dakota, where he made a fortune."

"Yes, and he earned it," Spies said. "I've often thought of that—the contrast—but I don't think he had any more fun than I did. We both had the same kind of fun. He made a game out of making money, and I made a game of other accomplishments. His paid off better, I guess." Spies chuckled. "When he died, he left an estate worth 3.7 million dollars from which I benefited greatly. Here I had all this schooling, and my estate would have been, if I had depended on myself, about a hundred thousand dollars." He laughed again. "It would have been nothing compared to his. And he only went to school through eighth grade. Isn't that interesting?"

"Very." I suspect most people would think an estate of a hundred thousand dollars was nothing to cry about. I asked, "You think the reason you were both successful is because you made a game out of it?"

Spies nodded enthusiastically. "Yes! You have to love what you do—that's the secret of it. Especially in chemistry. If a person takes chemistry, and he's not fascinated by it, why...he should just forget it. You can't make it."

I said, "I would like to know more about your family—your brothers and sisters—what they were like and how they affected you. Who would you say you were closest to?"

Spies paused, thinking. "Earl was the workaholic. Arthur was the oldest. He stayed in Madison, and he became an employee of the town, maintaining parks and doing the lawn and things like that. He worked for them his whole life practically."

"People who live in small towns often have to make sacrifices career-wise," I observed.

Spies said, "He never was ambitious like the rest of us. But it is probably thanks to Arthur that I received the little sex education that I did."

"He evidently felt some responsibility toward you."

"Yes, well, he was sort of a wild one when he was young. He used to go out with girls, and I don't know how much he knew."

"He evidently wanted to impart some wisdom to you," I said. "But what exactly do you mean by—sex education?"

Spies explained, "When I was in high school, sex was a taboo subject. Nobody had ever discussed it with me. Up to that point, my sex education consisted of seeing the mechanics of it performed by farm animals. The rest of it would consist of the appearance of a booklet entitled *BVP*, which stood for *Boys Venereal Peril*.

"The booklet just mysteriously appeared one day. I assume my brother Arthur put it where I would find it. He never spoke to me about it, so I never knew for sure." He laughed. "The booklet had a red cover. It was written in such graphic style that it scared the pants off of me. That I never had a date in high school was attributed to my shyness. Actually, I never dated all through my first year of college. And this had less to do with my shyness than it did with that book.

"My only romantic contact with girls up until then had consisted of that valentine the girl at school gave me when I was thirteen. Certainly, I had had no sexual contact of any kind. All of my information with regard to human sex came from this little book, *BVP*. And it served me well."

"Scared you to death for many years," I commented.

Spies said, "Yes. I was married in 1930 at twenty-six years of age."

I wasn't quite sure how to take that. Was he saying he would have gotten married earlier if he didn't have this fear? I don't think that's what he was saying. I think he was saying indirectly and possibly even unconsciously, that he was a virgin when he got married. That was one effective book.

Spies continued. "The fear of catching venereal disease was so powerful that it crossed over into the college years. I was so terrified that I remained a virgin all during college. After that, my sex life is private."

I asked, "You were dating after that first year?"

"Yes, we'll get into that a little bit." He laughed.

Generally, I don't think about scientists having personal lives—let alone sex lives. I suspect many people think the same thing about teachers or ministers, perhaps, because they seem like public domain. We see these people when they're working in their respective professions—not going out on a date or having an argument with one of their children or even something as mundane as emptying the garbage. We tend to see them only in the light of the their professions, and we place them on a pedestal of sorts. It is a shock when we find out personal details about their lives—discover they are human like us.

4

USD—1922

"My first year of college at USD," Spies said, "I lived off-campus with Lynn and Merlin Zenner from Wentworth, South Dakota. Lynn was a junior. He was going with my sister Helen at the time, and he later married her. Both Lynn and Helen became well respected teachers in Sioux Falls. I remember Helen taught elementary. They still are well known—Lynn especially. He's blind, but he takes bus trips and he gets around Sioux Falls. He's an amazing person. I telephone him regularly. He still lives in Sioux Falls." Spies smiled. "I remember vividly ...Lynn really knew the ropes at USD, and he was a big help to me in many ways.

"Going to college in those days was different than it is now. The only requirement was graduation from high school. There were no SAT scores. And you did not need to make arrangements ahead of time. You just appeared in the registration line and picked out your courses. I selected chemistry as my science requirement at random. Tuition was $6.50 a semester.

"That may sound cheap to anyone who has had to pay tuition in recent years, but financing was still a problem. My mother had left me about four to five hundred dollars inheritance. Together with what I made through odd jobs, I had enough to see me through my first year. I did yard jobs such as raking leaves and washing windows, and I worked as a substitute dishwasher at East Hall Dining Room. The football players had all of the jobs for dishwashing full-time. When they weren't there, I substituted for them. Lynn Zenner was head waiter at this dining room."

I said, "I was wondering what things you remember about what you did with them—your roommates, Lynn and Merlin."

Spies answered, "Lynn, who was the older one of the two brothers, was like a mentor. Since he was going with my sister, he took a special interest in me, and he'd show me all the ropes. For example, they advised me on what was called Freshman Day. And the night before that was sort of a hazing. Lynn and Merlin advised me not to go out because I was going to get into trouble if I did. I ignored their warnings and went out anyway." He chuckled.

I was puzzled. "Were freshmen easy to identify for some reason?"

"We had to wear green caps, distinctive caps," he said.

"The freshmen did? Anytime you went out you had to wear them?"

"Oh yes," Spies answered. "It was quite easy to spot the first-year students. I was soon captured."

"Who captured you?"

"Upperclassmen," he said. "And I remember the final thing they did in the morning before they let us go—they kept us out all night ..."

"What'd they do with you?" I asked.

He laughed. "Oh, minor tortures. The thing they did finally was to have us run the gauntlet. You had to run between two lines of people who had paddles and they would really hit you on your buttocks as you ran through. And they really meant business."

I said, "I thought they only used to do that in fraternities."

"No, this was the whole campus. Just that one night." He chuckled. "I felt a great deal of admiration for one freshman, who was a boxer. They would regularly hold boxing matches between freshmen and upperclassmen. Usually, the freshmen got pounded. And, of course, the upperclassmen who ran the match would cheat by putting big gloves on the freshmen so they couldn't hurt the upperclassmen. But this fellow was so good that he knocked out his opponent, even with the big gloves."

I said, "All the freshmen must have been cheering."

He laughed. "Yes, we were."

"What sort of outside activities did you do?"

Spies said, "I really didn't have much time for outside activities. I did teach Sunday School, but I didn't like it. I had trouble getting up and talking about the Bible. I just couldn't reconcile the whole thing. Many years later, I married a Methodist who attended church. She used to go by herself; I just couldn't do it.

"Lynn graduated, and I roomed with Merlin, the younger one, after he left. I remember they were having a parade. And he went down to sit on the porch and watch the parade in his pajamas because it was late at night. I turned on the porch light"—he laughed—"exposing him to the people in the parade. That first year we lived on Willow Street, right across from President Slagle's house.

"Then I think we lived on East Clark Street. I think we were west of where the library is now."

I asked, "Are there any other experiences from your freshman year that stand out in your mind?"

"No, not really," he said. "I'd been away from home since I was ten years old."

It's true—he was definitely not your typical college freshman. I asked, "What about your schoolwork at USD?"

Spies said, "My classwork went smoothly. My interest in chemistry started early in Dr. Haine's general chemistry class. One experiment was responsible for piquing my interest—the crystallization of alum. The formation and growth of these beautiful crystals fascinated me and stimulated a passion for chemistry that I never got over. That's what started it all—such a simple thing as that."

I asked, "Why did that fascinate you?"

"You had this solution, where everything was in water. And these crystals gradually formed. And they became huge. It was just that process, a very simple thing.

"I intended to continue my college career in chemistry, but my father became ill. He couldn't run his business by himself. I decided to stay out of school and run his business for him, for at least one year." He looked at me. "At the time I would have been nineteen, I guess."

I'm not so sure I would have quit school to help a father who had put me in an orphanage. "Was it difficult to leave school?"

He shrugged. "It didn't seem to be."

"You didn't feel like you were making a sacrifice?"

Amazingly, Spies said, "I thought I kind of owed it to him. Here again, a lot of people would have bearing a grudge for being put in the home and resenting it and obsessing over it all of their lives. I never did have one thought, never in my life thought about that."

Sitting across the table from him, studying him, I understood. Growing up in the Midwest makes you stoic, makes you tougher, even under the best of circumstances. He had very rough circumstances to endure. But, more significantly, Spies had his own sense of what it meant to be loyal. And if that meant leaving college to help his father out, that's what he would do.

5

Driving an Oil Truck and Dating

Dr. Spies began again, "My father was hard to know. He never talked much about his past. That may have been with good reason, because I believe one of his relatives—it might have been his brother—was hanged in the Haymarket Insurrection in Chicago—although he didn't tell me that. A paper was published in the Smithsonian. It had a picture of him, of this man that was hanged, and he looked just like my father. I imagine he didn't want to publicize that, at the time especially. I don't know for sure that it was him. But his name was Spies. And he looked like him. I had documentation on this but have misplaced it."

"It sounds as if it's a good possibility this is some relation. You also mentioned that you thought your father fled the relatives that he stayed with when he first came here."

Spies said, "That is sort of speculation. He left home when he was a young kid, probably. Twelve or thirteen years old."

Spies paused. "No, he came over here...he was born in Dusseldorf, Germany, and he came over here and stayed with a relative and he ran away from home...from that home. See, he was an independent cuss, too." Spies laughed.

I laughed too. "Yeah, that's where you get it."

It appears Spies' father was, in some sense, an orphan too. Although I could only speculate, he was definitely alienated from his family in Germany. It is not surprising then that he would think nothing of sending his own children away to an orphanage.

Spies continued, "My father ran the Standard Oil Bulk Station in Wentworth, South Dakota, a town of only a few hundred people. Actually, he worked for Standard Oil of Indiana. He worked for them in two periods—before he went on the farm, and after. In the earlier period, he used horses to drive his oil truck to nearby towns thirty miles away. Three horses, I think he used.

"The second time around, when he worked for Standard Oil of Indiana again, he delivered oil from a Model T truck with a 350 gallon capacity tank.

"Although I was only nineteen—as I said earlier—I agreed to stay out of school in 1923-24 to help my father. I loved to drive, so it was no burden to drive his truck for him."

I wasn't sure what he meant. He loved his father, so it was no burden to leave college and work for him? Or, he didn't mind helping his father out because he liked driving the oil truck? I believe he meant the second explanation.

Spies continued, "My father was getting worried about me because I never had a date during my first year of college."

I sat up, hearing this. "How so? Did he say something to you?"

Spies answered, "He would joke about it, but I think he meant it too. I guess he thought I might be homosexual or something. He only said he was worried about me; he didn't say why."

"Would he suggest girls, or point out girls, for you to go out with?"

Spies said, "My sister Ruth was attending high school in Wentworth at that time, and my father agreed to let me have his car if I would take Ruth and a girlfriend of hers to dances and so forth. This arrangement worked quite well. I lost my fear of girls. I learned to dance and enjoy the company of the opposite sex. And how I enjoyed it!" He laughed.

I observed, "That was pretty sneaky of your father." This side of his father surprised me.

Spies agreed, "Yes, it was." He chuckled. "He was thinking of me. My father gave me a hundred dollars a month to run the oil station. I saved money for a while, but as my social life increased, my savings decreased."

"You spent money on—what?"

Spies shrugged, smiled. "Well, you know how it is. I went to dances, spent money on girls and whatever else might come up.

"I worked as an assistant in bulk sales of petroleum products to farmers in the area, including Rutland to the north and Wentworth to the south. We had no strict boundaries. We measured gas in five-gallon pails. We ran it out of a faucet, with the pail hanging below it. You measured five gallons of gasoline, and then dumped that into the container." He looked at me. "Actually, I think it deformed me. I became high in one shoulder."

"Because you kept using the same motion over and over?"

"Yes," he said. "People who did this kind of work all of their lives actually did get deformed. During harvest and threshing time we were very busy; in the wintertime business slacked off.

"We drove mostly over dirt roads. This was good in dry weather, but difficult in wet weather. I had to drive the truck in low gear through the mud." He looked at me, smiling a little. "Did you ever drive a Model T Ford?"

I shook my head. "No. I had grandparents who did." It was startling to think how long ago Spies and my grandparents would have been driving these Model Ts—the 1920s.

Spies explained, "Because this was a Model T Ford truck, I had to press the low pedal all the time. This was very hard on the foot after I had driven for several hours. My foot used to hurt just terribly sometimes, because the more the motor worked, the harder I pressed. It was psychological. You didn't have to do that; but you just did it anyway, you know, psychologically."

I commented, "So it was a lot of work to drive a Model T."

"In wet weather it was," he answered. "I had to start the motor of the truck by hand cranking. This was very difficult and dangerous in the wintertime because of the stiffness of the motor. In the worst cases, this meant jacking up the back wheel and cranking to exhaustion. It was dangerous because, if the motor kicked, many people would get their hands or arms broken.

"One time I broke down and had to abandon my truck near Rutland. I came upon a train engine that had stopped for water. I approached the engineer and asked him if I could have a ride to the next town. I was surprised when he said yes. He actually let me ride in the cab of the engine—a steam engine. It was the only time I ever got to ride in the cab.

"Wintertime activities during the slack times consisted of playing cards in the pool hall, exchanging stories, and, of course, playing pool. I usually went to an American Legion dance about once a week. They had a little orchestra. They played jazz, mainly. I remember the Charleston came in just about that time."

I asked, "Did you dance the Charleston?"

"No, I couldn't." He shook his head emphatically, grinning. "My girlfriend could, but I couldn't."

"Would she drag you out on the dance floor anyway?"

Spies said, "No, she didn't try to." He laughed. "I should say—one of my girlfriends at that time."

"Did you have a favorite song or type of music you liked?"

"For dancing, I loved the waltz," he said. "I loved 'The Missouri Waltz.' And some waltzes written by an Austrian."

I asked, smiling, "How long did you stay there, working for your father—and going to dances?"

He answered, "I ran the station for thirteen months. My father never fully recovered, but he did get well enough to do work with another helper.

"I decided to go back to school. It was 1924. Once again, I could have gone on working, I suppose, and forfeited my college education. But I got my appetite whetted with that chemistry class, and I wanted to continue."

With what I already knew about Dr. Spies, I couldn't picture him not finishing what he had begun. That seemed to me to be a very Midwestern aspect of his character.

6

Slaving Away at USD and a ROTC Vacation

Dr. Spies told me he lived with the Fred Bergstresser family during the year he worked for his father. In the years that followed, home on visits from college, he would stay with them.

I asked, "Did you become pretty close to them?"

He nodded. "Pretty close, yes. Fred always liked his beer, and he was a hunter, you know."

I knew this was a sensitive area. "Were you still hunting at that time?"

"No," he said, "I didn't have time. I didn't want to do it, anyway, even then."

"So you were already changing over as far as your views of hunting were concerned?"

Spies answered, "Yes, I was. But my brother Earl never changed. He was a—" He laughed, sounding a bit exasperated "—a doggone hunter all his life."

"Did you debate it with him?"

"No," he said, "I thought it was futile."

Perhaps, this was a case of a younger brother bowing to an older's brother's authority. He did have a great deal of respect for Earl.

Spies continued, "I supported myself solely by working. By my junior year in college I was regularly waiting tables in East Hall for my board. I received ten dollars per month for taking ROTC, and this covered my room rent. I spent all of my extra time working in the state chemistry lab under Guy G. Frary, the state chemist. Carl Stone worked there too. Of course, Frary was the head of it. I worked for 40 cents an hour." He laughed. "Big deal. But it was great for me."

"What were your duties?" I asked.

"Oh, I mostly tested gasoline and kerosene samples that came into the state," he said. "They had to meet certain specifications. That was my main thing that I did. I worked on Saturday afternoons. I'd hear the football players and the cheers going up while I was working. I don't think I went to a single ballgame."

I tried to picture what his life at USD must have been like. "Did you say you lived in the dorms?"

He answered, "No, I never lived in a dormitory—thank goodness."

"So you worked at this job—did it pay all your bills?"

He explained, "This job at the state lab gave me cash for clothes and other essentials. Through summer vacations I worked on either Lawrence Graf's farm or at his brother's...Frank Graf's. In this way I was able to finance my education. I had to borrow only $100 from the Harmon Loan Foundation in my whole time at school."

I could tell he was proud of the fact that he had borrowed only $100 for his schooling.

He continued, "I spent these three years in hard work. I had little time for social life but was content to make a living and go to school, studying under Dr. Pierce, Dr. Haines, and Dr. Pardee."

He looked at me then. "Incidentally, I did not join a fraternity. I was asked, but I wasn't asked the first year. I was asked during the second year when they saw..." —his voice grew cynical — "...when they saw that I got good grades in science, and they wanted me for that purpose. I didn't want to join. I was an independent. And my whole life I disliked fraternities. My son joined a fraternity when he went to college, but that's beside the point. He's another generation."

He laughed, obviously pleased that he had brought this up. I didn't find his dislike of fraternities surprising. Being in a fraternity does tend to encourage a similar way of doing things and thinking, and I couldn't see Joseph Spies feeling comfortable in such an environment.

Dr. Spies continued, "I was taking chemistry and had many afternoon laboratories. It was extremely tricky to juggle my morning classes, working in the dining room at lunch time, and then attending labs in the afternoon. As soon as I finished my morning classes, I would rush over to East Hall and work during lunch time. I would hurriedly eat something and clean my table where eight people had been sitting for lunch. Then I would get ready for class and rush off to my afternoon labs, usually held at one-thirty."

I commented, "Your schedule sounds horrible. I don't know how you managed to function."

Spies nodded. "I had to do all that, which was really a terrible thing for a young undergraduate. You never could relax. It helped me over this time that I loved chemistry so much—I think this is necessary to succeed in a subject as difficult as chemistry."

"So you feel these rough early experiences built character?"

"Yes," he said. "It was almost too much for me, though. My one pleasure during those rushed lunch times would be waiting on this one particular girl."

I stopped taking notes and stared at Dr. Spies, surprised. "Really?"

Spies nodded. "She always ate at the table to which I was assigned as a waiter. I used to give her special desserts." He smiled. "The other girls didn't seem to mind. I think they understood I had a soft spot for her.

"My main handicap, of course, would come back to haunt me during these college years. I had no time to learn or no one to teach me the social graces."

I said, "So you didn't have time to socialize. Did you ever resent the fact that all these people around you were socializing or having fun?"

"No," he said, shaking his head. "They were there to make more friends than me and get along."

"Did you have any social disasters?"

"As a matter of fact, I did. My lack of social skills was most manifest in the spring of 1926. It was announced in General Assembly that I had been elected to Phi Beta Kappa. At the time, when they announced it, I was shooting baskets in the gymnasium. But if that wasn't bad enough ....

"I was then sent a written invitation to attend a reception for all Phi Beta Kappa electees, and not only did I not go to the reception, I did not even send a note declining. Believe me, I have since learned that this is not acceptable behavior!" He laughed at his own faux pas. "I heard that the person that gave the reception was a little bit teed off about it, but, they didn't withdraw my election to Phi Beta Kappa—which I was grateful for."

I could see why Dr. Spies felt self-conscious about this, but I had to smile to myself. Can you imagine the people at Phi Beta Kappa withdrawing Spies' election and electing someone else instead, not because they deserved it, but because they had better social skills?

Dr. Spies continued with his narrative. "In the summer of 1926, I had a brief adventure in the ROTC. We were sent to ROTC Camp for six weeks at Fort Snelling in Minneapolis, Minnesota. War was not on the horizon, so I did not take this too seriously. A group of us drove together to the camp, which was like a vacation to me. However, I did manage to get into some trouble.

"It all started when a stack of arms in my squad fell down. The front rank made the stack. I was in the rear rank, and so, I did not feel responsible. The leader in our squad was Dwight Redfield, a college basketball player. He was evidently trying to make a name for himself in ROTC. He told the squad to practice stacking arms during lunch time. I refused. This was a mistake."

Spies laughed and continued. "The commanding officer, a captain who was a regular military man, punished me by forcing me to learn the stack arms procedure verbatim and to recite it every morning at revelry until the end of camp. I obeyed this order and became known as Stack-Arms Spies, a nickname which followed me back to South Dakota."

I smiled, wondering if anyone still called Dr. Spies by this name. "That's a great story."

ROTC unit in camp at Fort Snelling, MN, 1926.
Spies is second from left, back row.

Spies continued. "Another time, we were occupying a hill, which overlooked a terrain where the 'enemy' was supposed to be advancing. The enemy was so exposed that I casually said to my fellow soldiers, 'I'd hate to give the order to shoot these people.'

"I don't know whether people would enjoy giving an order like that or not." Some of my fellow soldiers, my 'friends,' reported me to the commanding officer. For my remarks, casually made, I was severely reprimanded. He said he'd kick me out of the ROTC if I didn't shape up.

"Now, here's another thing I did that was very stupid and showed poor judgment. Purely on a lark, I signed up for a boxing match.

"I was a wiry young man but no match for a trained athlete. I'd had a little practice. I got a draw out of one match. Except for practice, that was my sole experience in boxing. And I was foolish enough to think that my opponent and I would get in there and lightly spar.

"When I got into the ring with this boxer, it was a disaster. In a match like this, my opponent meant business—as well he should. His objective was to knock me out.

"I landed flat on my back after about fifteen seconds of the first round. When he hit me, I didn't feel anything, and I jumped right up. But from then on, I was in a desperate survival mode for the rest of the bout—no thanks to the referee, who continually urged me to 'get in there and fight!' I felt like telling him, 'If you think it's so much fun, you go ahead and take it. I've had enough.' "

Spies laughed, shaking his head. "I just grabbed my opponent and hung on to him for the rest of the match, for three rounds. Because he was merciful, I survived.

"After the fight, I made a point to seek out the boxer and thank him for not killing me, which I am sure he could have done. We parted friends, but I had a headache for a week afterwards."

I observed with some teasing, "That was the end of your boxing career."

"It really was," he said. "It was the most stupid thing that I've ever done—or at least one of the most," he corrected himself. "At the end of ROTC Camp, I had to make a crucial decision: whether I would quit school and go north to a lumber camp to work or if I would continue in school for my last year. I had paid off a small debt, which left me almost without funds for school."

I asked, astonished, "You were thinking of going to a lumber camp?"

"Yes," he responded. "That's rather romantic, you know. Really, I just thought I would go north and get a job. But I decided I would have a go at school instead. I took a bus to Sacred Heart, Minnesota, where I got a job harvesting wheat. I worked until it was time to go back to school.

"The bus ticket to Vermillion just about wiped out my funds. I did not have enough money to register and pay tuition. To make matters worse, tuition had gone up. Later, I figured it out—it had increased 400 percent since my freshman year, from $6.50 a semester to $25.00.

"I decided to start classes without registering until I got my first check from the state chemistry lab. This worked out just fine for about a month. But then I received a notice from Mr. Julian to register and pay my admission fees. I ignored the first notice and received a second one which said, 'Pay up or leave school.'

"I then went to Mr. Julian's office and explained the situation. He was very kind to me. We worked out some type of arrangement for deferring payment until I got my first paycheck. So I got through this minor emergency, although I was always just on the edge of bankruptcy, so to speak." And he laughed.

I was amazed at Joseph Spies' resourcefulness and determination to continue with school in those lean years of the 1920s. Most people would have have given up under those circumstances, but Dr. Spies proved his determination to face whatever life handed him without rancor and with determination.

7

The Hobo Years

Spies said, "After graduation in 1927, I had a temporary job at the state chemistry lab in Vermillion, working full-time in Kjeldal nitrogen determinations. Actually, I had a life professional diploma in education, but I did not wish to teach. I had a baby face, which would have made keeping discipline quite difficult for me, anyway.

"During that summer, I started dating the girl who sat at my dining table in East Hall. She was attending summer school."

Ah ha. I wondered when we were going to get back to her. I leaned forward to listen more closely.

He continued, "This turned out to be a case of unrequited love—or, at least, I thought so at the time. I really fell for her, but she turned me down. I felt so strongly about it, I was devastated. After I left USD, I would not hear from her again for a couple of years."

I was stunned at hearing him express these feelings. It seemed like the sort of thing the emotionally conservative Dr. Spies would never reveal.

Spies continued, "That's when I decided to go to California. It really didn't have anything to do with this girl. I would have gone on the trip anyway. I certainly didn't have illusions of becoming a movie star or anything like that. But, to a South Dakotan,"—his voice deepened with surprising emotion—"California was the land of golden dreams. If I could get out there, things were going to be better.

"I bought a stripped-down Ford car for thirty-five dollars. It had no top, no fenders, and half a windshield, but it ran. I was going to go with a...I'm not going to name this fellow," (he said this as if the man in question had committed a crime) "he didn't show up—a man from Vermillion. He backed out of the trip before we got started. I decided to go alone.

"I knew I would have to work on the way because I did not have enough money for the trip. I started out early in the morning and got to Vivian, South Dakota the first day. It's across the Missouri River, west of Pierre. I got a job in a hay baling camp there, north of town. The job lasted two weeks. I made friends with two men there, one from Vivian, the other from some place in Iowa. We decided to head north for wheat harvesting. We ended up in Newburg, North Dakota, close to the Canadian border. First we got a job in shocking wheat. Do you know what shocking wheat is?"

I pictured running up behind several innocent, unsuspecting stalks of wheat and yelling, "Fire!" but I said only, "No—what is shocking wheat?"

"We had to cut grain with a machine that tied it into bundles," he explained. "We had to set the bundles on their ends so that the wheat part wouldn't get wet and rot the grain when it rained. Then we would pitch these bundles into hay racks for threshing, pitching them into threshing machines. This was hard work. We got top wages for the times, though—sixty cents per hour. We worked from sunrise to sunset. At night, we slept in a barn-like building."

I asked, "Now, all this time you were working at the different jobs, different places—did you have any adventures or was it all work?"

"Oh no." he said, "We went to dances and so forth on Saturday nights. Oh yes, we also played poker when it was raining and we couldn't work—small stakes, of course."

"Sounds like a great way to lose your earnings."

"As a matter of fact, I usually won, but—I won because I knew when to lay down." He chuckled. "When to fold. We didn't play high stakes, anyway."

"Wasn't this the Prohibition Era?"

"Yes."

"So you couldn't have spent your money on drinking?" I said this sort of tongue-in-cheek, but Dr. Spies took it seriously.

He said in a lowered voice, "I'm afraid I learned the hazards of drinking homemade liquor the hard way. One night at a dance, I drank some Canadian whiskey. I didn't have very much, actually. I believe it was poisoned. I got horribly sick. It nearly killed me, I think, really.

"My friends dumped me in the back of a pickup truck and took me home. I was really out of it. It was touch and go whether I would live or not. That really did me a favor because I lost my taste for liquor and didn't touch it for a long time after that."

Horrified, I said, "I think that would do it for me too."

Spies smiled, his mood lightening a bit. "It taught me a lesson, and I avoided drinking for a long time. Another interesting thing happened—and it's amazing—it comes under the heading of 'small world'...a fellow from Madison, South Dakota by the name of Harry Dirkson showed up opposite me, pitching bundles. He said, 'Hi, Joe.' " Spies chuckled.

"I didn't recognize him at first and then it dawned on me who he was. Harry was headed for Europe. He was sort of an artist. He wanted to get experience over there."

"So he was saving his money for a trip to Europe?"

Spies smiled wryly. "Yeah. Well— he wasn't saving enough because he jumped ship when he got to Europe."

I could detect stern Midwestern judgment in Spies' voice— then he added, "Harry was adventurous" as if that made up for Harry's jumping ship in Spies' mind.

Spies resumed with his tale. "My two friends and I stayed in North Dakota until the middle of October. Then we got on the road. We dropped off my friend from Iowa, and the chap from Vivian, South Dakota stayed with me on the trip to California. His name was George Stolley.

"We travelled west through the Badlands where...," his voice became warmer, "the first time I saw the Badlands, I fell in love with them. Into Wyoming, Colorado, and New Mexico."

I asked, "What was it that struck you about the Badlands when you first saw them?"

"Oh, I thought they were fantastic!" he exclaimed. "The formations were just—I'd never seen anything like that. Many years later, I came out from Maryland and spent a whole week just taking pictures of the Badlands. I was very much inspired by them.

"Then we came to a place called Ratoon Pass, where we met two Jewish boys from New York, who, just like us, were traveling to California. And they were having some trouble with their car. It was similar to ours but a later model—a Ford. And, just like us, they were running out of money.

"They didn't know much about cars, and George and I didn't know a lot more. These New York boys thought you had to adjust the carburetor to correct for high elevation. Maybe you do, but I had never heard of that before and never have since.

"Because the lights weren't working on their car, we offered to lead the way. We drove down the Ratoon Pass, which is a high mountain between Colorado and New Mexico, in the evening. Since they didn't have any lights, they followed us very closely."

Spies paused. "You know, with those old Fords, the brightness of the lights depended on how fast the motor was running. When the motor was running slow, you hardly had any lights to see by.

"We drove down this narrow mountain pass with the two boys from New York behind us in their car, ours with dim lights because we were driving slowly, theirs with none at all." He laughed, shaking his head.

"Anyway, when we got to Ratoon, the boys from New York sold their car, which gave them a little money. They then travelled the rest of the way with us.

"We now had to cross New Mexico and Arizona before reaching California. It gets surprisingly cold in the desert at night, and our new friends were not dressed for it. They were dressed for city life, for milder weather. They were so miserable from the cold that they practically cried." He looked at me earnestly. "It's cold as the dickens at night in the desert. We got to a town called Holbrook, Arizona—I'll never forget the name—" he chuckled—"where we went into a hotel. Of course, we had no intentions of renting a room. We had very little money. We just didn't want to sleep outside—it was freezing cold.

"It was about twelve midnight when we came into the hotel, and the lobby was sort of closed. But there was a nice, cozy fire in there. The four of us sat around this fire to get warm and— naturally—dozed off.

"About dawn, an old lady came downstairs into the lobby and saw us sleeping around the fire. She grabbed up a poker and immediately started beating us. She meant to either hurt us or kill us. I remember I held my arm up to protect myself. Later, I saw I had welts along my arm. Some of the fellows got hit on the head even. Then she shouted, 'You dirty bums, get out of here!' And so we did."

I observed, "She thought you were vagabonds."

"Yes," he said. "So we left in a hurry. One fellow left his hat in there, and she fired it out into the middle of the street." Spies laughed.

I tried to put myself in this irate innkeeper's shoes. "Boy, she must have had some previous bad experiences."

"Oh, I'm sure she did," he said. "When we started out again, we saw a fire in a depot that was on the railroad track. We went there to ask them if we could come in and get warm and they said no. So we were out in the cold from then on.

"We had just enough money to buy gasoline, but that was about all. We decided we would each eat only one quarter loaf of bread per day for the rest of the trip. We went into a store to buy our loaf of bread one time—I think this was the second day. We were terribly hungry. I remember I put the loaf of bread on the counter to pay for it.

"The fellow behind the counter said, 'Don't you want any meat with that?'

"One of us answered, 'Yeah, we'd sure like it, but we don't have any money.'

"He gave us a ring of baloney, just gave it to us. So there was some kindness too, on this trip. We appreciated it very much."

Spies continued. "We got to Los Angeles finally and parted with our New York friends. We never saw them again. They claimed to have some relatives there, in Los Angeles.

"We found a cheap hotel where George and I could stay. We also discovered a Japanese restaurant where we could get meals for fifteen cents." He looked intently at me. "Now that doesn't seem possible, does it?"

"It's pretty cheap." Even for that time it seemed dirt cheap. Spies chuckled. "We devoured every scrap of the meals and even took the leftover bread with us."

Here were these two young men from the Midwest in a strange place, living on what little money they had, in a shaky 1920s economy. I asked, "Were you able to get work?"

Spies nodded. "I got a job through an employment agency. The job was on a sheep ranch in the Pacific Ocean on San Clemente Island, which is about twenty miles farther out than Catalina Island. This ranch had about 20,000 sheep and 5,000 goats which ran wild. They were left by the Spaniards that had lived there previously."

Spies' typically stoic expression became downright euphoric as he remembered that place from his youth. "Seeing the Pacific Ocean for the first time, I was greatly thrilled. I remember I went swimming on New Year's Day, just so I could say that I had done it. The water was actually quite comfortable."

"What did you do at the sheep ranch?" I asked.

"My first job was to guard a waterhole at sea level from marauding fishermen," Spies said. "The fishermen got tired of eating fish, so they would come into this place and kill some sheep for food. During the dry season, the sheep had to come there to drink. When the rainy season started a little later than that, there would be water, so they wouldn't have to come down to this waterhole.

"The waterhole was right at the bottom of the hill which was right on the ocean. There was a little campsite there, twelve miles from the ranch house, also at sea level, at the foot of this 2,000-mile-high mountain.

"My boss gave me a .44 caliber pistol and a .30 caliber Winchester rifle. I asked him, 'Am I expected to shoot at anybody?' He said, 'Use your own judgment.'

"I decided I would not shoot anyone." Spies laughed.

"Geez," I said, "why the gun, I wonder?"

Spies explained,"Before I came to work at the ranch, there had been a feud between the fishermen and one of the ranch hands. This ranch hand had shot a bullet into a fisherman's boat, and the fisherman became furious. He swore he was going to kill somebody for that. I didn't know any of this when I went to guard the watering hole."

I asked, "Did you have confrontations with any fishermen?"

"No, I never saw one," Spies answered. "And it's rather interesting. My very first night at the camp, I heard stones bounding down the hill and over my tent." He laughed. "The sheep, evidently, were kicking the stones downhill. In theory, the stones wouldn't hit the tent; they would just jump over it. This made me very uncomfortable, worrying about these rocks, which in my mind had become huge boulders. Understandably, I had a lot of trouble sleeping. Imagine how much more trouble I would have had if I had known about the fisherman bent on revenge." He laughed again.

"One of my other duties out there was to shear any woolly sheep that had been missed in the regular shearing. The first

Spies at the California sheep ranch in 1928. Note the pistol.

sheep that I tried to shear—the first woolly—it was really a wrestling match. It took me about an hour, and I just couldn't— I didn't know how to do it."

"Had anyone shown you how to do it?"

"No, no. They didn't show me how or anything. Really professional people can shear a sheep in a matter of minutes. The secret, as I learned later, is to put the sheep on his bottom so his feet are off the ground. That way he can't use them as leverage. Do you know what I mean?"

It was hard not to smile, as I imagined Dr. Spies struggling with this sheep. "Yes, I think so."

Spies continued, "If he gets his feet on the ground, he can make a great wrestling match out of it—which that first sheep did. He got lots of nicks and cuts." He chuckled. "I was exhausted, but I did shear him. Later, I learned how to shear properly, although we didn't have much of that type of work to do."

He paused, obviously thinking. "It's funny—I had my A.B. degree from the University of South Dakota and I was qualified in both chemistry and teaching. And here I was on this island in the Pacific, sheepherding, guarding a watering hole.

"Sitting out there, I had a lot of time to think about what I wanted. I decided, if I ever did get a job in chemistry—if I could make use of my chemistry—I would be happy to do the best I could. No matter how low the job was. That I would just be satisfied. I aspired to get up to P-3, which was professional grade three. That paid three thousand dollars a year at that time. And I thought, well, if I ever get up there, I'll be just fine. I'll be content to stay there the rest of my life." Spies laughed, shaking his head in wonderment. "It sounds foolish to me now, but—that's the way I felt about it."

I observed, "It was really probably that attitude that got you where you were. How long did you stay out there guarding the sheep?"

"I stayed at the camp for about twelve days," Spies said, "until it rained. Then I went back to the ranch house, walking the whole twelve miles. I was glad to get out of there. If I had known at that time about the shooting incident between the ranch hand and the fisherman, why, I think I would have counted myself very lucky to have returned unharmed."

I said, smiling, "Aren't you glad you heard about it—afterward?"

"Yes, yes," he said, laughing. "That would have been one more thing, with the stones bounding over my head."

We both lost it. Dr. Spies was shaking with laughter. I said, "That's actually, funny. AFTER—"

"It is," he agreed. When we were ready to resume, I asked, "What was your friend George doing while you were at the ranch?"

Spies' face was still red from laughing, but he quickly gained control. "I got George Stolley a job at the ranch too, after I had been there a short time. He had been working in a place that packaged nuts, earning less money."

I asked curiously, "Where did you sleep? Did all the ranch hands sleep in the same place?"

"Yes. In a bunkhouse," he said. "It was located right on the ocean beach. We could hear the ocean at night. And you know how soothing it is to hear the ocean.

"During the day, though, the ranch was a very rough place. It was cut off by a canyon, and there were huge cactus plants everywhere." He grinned. "One fellow had the misfortune to fall off his horse and land right on a cactus by accident, which, fortunately, I didn't do.

"And we rode horses everywhere. The idea was that a horse could go anywhere a man could, but the man wouldn't have to use his hands. However, I did get off my horse and walk some. Some of us would, although we were right on the edge of cliffs."

"So there were dangerous places."

"Extremely dangerous," he agreed. "There were narrow passes. And canyons."

I shook my head. "Boy. That sounds as if you should have been paid plenty."

Spies laughed. "Well, I don't remember what we did get paid out there, but it was a little bit more than what we got back in North Dakota."

I asked, "What other sort of work did you have to do on the ranch—besides actually herding and guarding the sheep?"

"One job on this ranch consisted of building a six-mile fence, another of building an earthen dam. To build the dam, we used a team of horses and a—what do you call it—a scoop pulled by horses. This took a long time, but we finally got the dam built. Later, the dam sprung a leak. If a dam like that—an earthen dam—starts to leak, you can't stop it. It finally went out with a terrible rush of water."

"Were you working there still, when it happened?"

"Yes, we saw it go out."

He smiled, remembering something else. "At that time, I used to smoke cigarettes. We were in a roundup riding horses and rounding up sheep, and when it got dark, we were too far away from the ranch house to go back. We had to go without eating that night. I was very happy to have cigarettes because, strangely enough, at that time I would rather have smoked cigarettes than eat."

"You're kidding," I exclaimed.

Spies shook his head. "No, I'm not. I quit in 1930, so I've been off cigarettes for a long time. But I did smoke at that time."

I asked, "Do you remember what kind of cigarettes you smoked?"

"Camels and Lucky Strikes, mostly." He chuckled. "You're probably familiar with Joe Camel, aren't you? I'd walk a mile for a Camel."

I smiled. "How long did you work at the sheep ranch?"

"George and I worked there until February, 1928. That's when we decided to return to South Dakota. I sold my car for almost nothing. Paying for parking the car while I spent several months at the ranch almost ate up what little money I did get. It was a good car, considering I only paid thirty-five bucks for it."

"That's pretty cheap," I commented.

"It's rather remarkable that it did get me to California for traveling. I never had any trouble with it."

I asked, "So, how did you get back?"

"George and I took a Jackrabbit bus back to South Dakota," Spies answered. "There, we parted company. He went back to Vivian and worked as a farm laborer."

"What about you?"

"I got a job working on a farm near Wentworth, South Dakota, staying there until I went back to school."

"Where'd you go to school?"

Spies answered, "The University of Maryland at College Park."

He added slowly, "Some part of me knew that this would be a permanent leaving of South Dakota and my family. I remember saying good-bye to my little sister Ruth, who was teaching eight grades in a one-room schoolhouse at the time, in a little town called Junius, west of Madison.

"I would never return to South Dakota to live, only for visits after that. I always loved to come out there. I remember on one particular visit how the sky suddenly seemed to open up. Here in D.C. you cannot see it. No...I never deserted them in spirit."

He was silent for a moment. Then, unexpectedly, he added, "Years later, I found a diary I wrote during my 'hobo period.' I threw it out."

I gasped, thinking of all of my own journals/diaries, carefully preserved from childhood on. "You did? You threw it out?"

"It had some cuss words in it and so forth." He laughed. "So I'm glad I threw it out myself because—"

I couldn't keep myself from interrupting this time. "I think it's a crime. You should never—"

"You should never write it in the first place." Spies finished my sentence for me, laughing. "You know what happened to Nixon."

8

A South Dakotan in Maryland

"When I first came to Washington, D.C. from South Dakota in 1928, I travelled by train. I arrived in College Park, Maryland after two days. Despite my years of roaming, I was more homesick than I had ever been.

"I ran into a college chum of my mine, Ron Stevens, whose father was a professor at USD. He took me to a movie, which eased my homesickness a bit.

"On the street at College Park, a stranger came up and asked me where a particular address was. He was new to the area, a student like myself. We struck up a conversation. I learned that he was from Bedford, Pennsylvania and his name was Thomas D. Smith. He and I ended up rooming together. Tom and I became lifelong friends."

I had been thinking hard about something and decided to interrupt. "I have a question for you that's off the topic —"

"That's all right."

"You had mentioned that you are an agnostic, which I found interesting. Were you always agnostic?"

Spies considered the question for a minute. "Well, I was baptized Baptist. My mother was quite religious. So she tried to instill religion. But when I got to thinking—" He leaned forward, clasping his hands on the table. "—now I had a roommate who one time—I used to worry about the veracity of the Bible. And you know, there's no way to solve it, really. My roommate at the University of Maryland told me that, 'It's just so simple.' He said, 'If God meant for you to know that, he'd have made it very plain. So you might just as well quit thinking about the afterlife and all that.' Which I proceeded to do. I took his advice on that."

This solution seemed very logical, although it was a little too nice and neat for me. "That's an interesting approach."

"Well, it's true, isn't it?" he asked.

"You can torment yourself," I observed, "and many people have."

Spies nodded. "I did—for many years."

I raised my head from my notes to look at him directly. I had trouble picturing Dr. Spies tormenting himself over the existence of God. "At what point did you know you were an agnostic?"

Spies frowned, evidently trying to remember. "Gradually, over the years, I finally decided—I don't go around preaching that I'm an agnostic. That's not one of the things that I'm proudest of, but in all honesty, I have to say that I hope there's an afterlife, but I rather doubt it. That's where I stand."

"Okay," I said. I realized he was done with this subject. "Back to your starting out in Maryland...."

Spies consulted his notes. "I was having a tough time financially. My father gave me a hundred dollars to help out during this time, for which I signed a promissory note. This was supposed to be part of his estate. He ended up cutting out my name from the note, which touched me deeply. It meant I didn't have to pay that money back. The note—he cut my name out."

"He just gave you the hundred dollars?"

"Yes. I signed the note for it when I got it, but he really gave it to me. He cancelled the note."

I said, "You mentioned your father had been ill. When did he die?"

Spies answered, "The illness my father had when I quit college that one time, to help him out with his business—that never went away. He eventually died of pneumonia in 1940, I believe, in Hot Springs, Arkansas. That's where he would spend his winters."

"To get away from harsh South Dakota weather?"

"Yes," he said patiently.

He wanted to get on with the telling of his early years in Maryland. "So how did you get on then at the University of Maryland?"

"I got a fellowship at the University," he said. "I worked in the chemistry department for fifty dollars a month as a graduate assistant. My board, room, and laundry amounted to forty-eight dollars, leaving me two dollars to live on."

I said disbelievingly, "Two bucks to live on—for a month?"

Spies laughed at my astonished expression. "Yes. Fortunately, another scholarship opened up for one hundred dollars a month, which temporarily solved my financial problems.

"I had chosen inorganic chemistry as my major for a Ph.D., but I decided I liked organic chemistry better. So I changed majors. This caused a little bit of friction between the professors, but not much."

I asked, "Why did you change? What made you switch from inorganic chemistry to organic chemistry?"

He shrugged his shoulders. "I thought it was more promising. The future of inorganic chemistry didn't look very promising to me. Organic chemistry did. I worked on insecticides during this period.

"Once again, I was guilty of stupidity, I think, although it worked out all right in the end. When spring came, my roommate Tom and I both decided we didn't know if we had done a satisfactory job in our scholarships or not. We didn't know whether we were going to be renewed for another year. We decided to take the Civil Service Examinations. We went over to Baltimore, Maryland and took the exams. I scored, since I was in graduate school, a plus 96 on it—there were several exams—and

I had one 98.8 in organic chemistry. And I think I averaged about 96 plus.

"I got an offer of a job almost at once. The first offer I had was at a munitions plant where the previous employee holding that position had been killed by a premature explosion." He laughed. "I decided not to take that job.

"Instead, I took one in the Chemical Warfare Service at Edgewood Arsenal, which is twenty to thirty miles north of Baltimore. They tested poisonous gases."

I commented, "That doesn't sound any safer."

Spies laughed again. "It is safer than blowing up."

"Edgewood Arsenal ...is that somehow connected to —"

"That was a Civil Service detail," Spies said, anticipating my question. "So I was working for the federal government instead of the University of Maryland, as a chemist. My friend Tom, who had taken the Civil Service Exams with me, decided to stay on at the University of Maryland as a student. He would go on to get a Ph.D. in chemistry."

"What year was this? 1928? '29?"

Spies said, "Let's see. Twenty—wait a minute. Yeah, it was '29."

"Didn't you get married around this time?"

He smiled. "I was just coming to that. While I was at Edgewood, I met my wife, who was then a secretary in one of the adjoining labs. Her folks lived in Edgewood. Her father, Joseph H. Numbers, was a station master for Pennsylvania Railroad."

Admiration crept into his voice. "Renice was a real scrimper and saver. She had saved her money while working as a secretary and living at home. She had more money than I ever did."

"Was it love at first sight?"

Spies shook his head. "No, not at first sight. It was gradual."

"And did she accept right away when you proposed?"

"No, she was a little bit hesitant. She might have been hesitant"—he laughed "—because of my checkered past, I guess."

I laughed too. Spies's past didn't strike me as checkered at all. Colorful, but certainly not checkered or anything to be ashamed of.

He continued, "Renice's family treated me like a son—better than I deserved to be treated, really. When we told her parents we wanted to get married, Renice's mother offered me an expensive wedding or a new car. Being a practical individual, I chose the car, a new Ford.

"Interestingly enough, about this time, I heard from my old girlfriend in South Dakota."

I was wondering when the old girlfriend was going to come up. Somehow, I knew that romantic episode in Dr. Spies' life wasn't over.

Spies continued, "She was teaching out in Colorado. I think she hinted that she would like to have me back in effect. The way I replied was that I was getting married. You know, just bluntly. I suppose I was still smarting a little from her initial rejection, although I had gotten over her. I could have handled that situation a little better.

"Renice and I were married on—she'd kill me—I hesitate, mentioning when we got married, because it was November 26, 1930."

I stared at him, trying to understand the hidden scandal. "Right after Thanksgiving?"

Spies nodded slightly, as if he were ashamed of this. "I took the whole time—that day and the weekend as a honeymoon. Can you imagine? That was the extent of my—my funds." He laughed ruefully. "We were married at a minister's home in Baltimore. It was a private ceremony; only Renice's father and mother attended. I didn't even notify my folks out in South Dakota when I got married, didn't invite them to the wedding or anything. I got married first and then told them afterwards."

"How did they react? Were they surprised?"

"I don't know if they were or not," he said. His surprised tone conveyed that he was considering this for the first time.

"But I'd been on my own so long, I just figured it was none of their business." He chuckled. "I didn't have the social graces."

It struck me then that Spies, for all his claims to be lacking in the "social graces," was more thoughtful than most people are about old relationships. More than sixty years later, he regretted his behavior toward that young woman. What was unusual (but not surprising, knowing what I did of Spies by now), was that he would not have let his family know about the wedding beforehand. Certainly, he fulfilled family obligations when he felt it was appropriate—such as quitting school temporarily to help his father—but that did not fall into the category of family closeness—of doing something out of love for blood relation.

I asked, "After you were married, did you continue on at Edgewood?"

Spies shook his head. "Not for long. The year 1929 was, of course, when the stock market crashed and the Great Depression officially began. People were being laid off from the jobs, and things were quite precarious. I stayed at Edgewood for one year"—he smiled, pausing for dramatic effect—"until I got an offer I couldn't refuse."

9

Earning the Ph.D. and Married Life

Spies consulted his notes. "Quite unexpectedly, I got an offer to come back to the University of Maryland at College Park to continue my schooling. It so happened that another South Dakotan had preceded me, and there was a general consensus that South Dakotans didn't know enough not to work very hard at what they did." He laughed. "I was also offered a position working at the Bureau of Entomology and Plant Quarantine."

"And this was where?" I asked.

"At the College Park in Maryland," he said. "The theory was that I could continue my graduate studies and work for the Bureau as well.

"The Bureau had a new technique that they wanted to develop, called microanalytical procedure by Pregl's Methods. This technique required about one-thousandth's amount of sample at least. Previously, it had been required for doing analysis of carbon, hydrogen, nitrogen, and so forth. This would now be useful to people working on the determination of the structure of rotenone, a new plant insecticide. I was the only chemist in the Washington area doing that kind of analysis, so I became quite valuable.

"I just went to classes as I had always done and did this work at the same time, which was a great thing for me. I was getting two thousand dollars a year, which was the starting salary of a professional grade chemist. In addition, because I was working for the government, they paid for all of my equipment. The other graduate assistants depended upon the equipment the University purchased, which, naturally, fell considerably short of what the Bureau could provide, although it was typically what a university would have. I was getting twice as much as the other graduate assistants, in terms of both pay and equipment." He laughed, sounding a bit cocky. "I really had it good."

"How about your wife—was she still working at Edgewood Arsenal?"

"No, she came to live with me then," he answered. "She never worked outside the home again." He said this with a certain old-fashioned pride, then added quickly, "She had been an excellent secretary—they were sorry to see her go at Edgewood."

"Where did you live?"

"In Riverdale, Maryland. We rented the upstairs of a house that an older couple owned, located near the University.

"So that was the way I spent the Depression—studying to get my M.S. and Ph.D. degrees and working as well. I'd had such a tough time before, that the Depression didn't seem...it seemed to be normal conditions." He looked at me questioningly. "You know what I mean?"

"Yes. You were used to living on very little and working very hard."

Spies nodded. "I know it was tough on Renice, but during those hard times, I would tell her, 'Remember the pioneers.'" He laughed. "That was one of my favorite expressions.

"I earned my M.S. degree in 1931 and continued on for my Ph.D. in organic chemistry. At the same time, I was also elected to Sigma Xi, an honorary fraternity, at the University of Maryland."

"When was Carl born?"

Spies flinched a little, startled by this personal question. "Let me see...a year later, in 1932, I think. Yes, I remember—at that particular time, I was studying for an examination in organic chemistry. I was really oblivious to everything else; I had to be."

Curious, I asked, "So you weren't a nervous wreck when you were about to become a father?"

"Well —" he laughed, embarrassed. "I took Renice to the hospital when it was time for the birth. Carl was born in Columbia Hospital, which was a hospital for women in Washington, D.C. And, I have to confess, while she was in labor, I was studying for the exam." He laughed at himself.

I grinned, inquiring, "Were you present for the actual birth of your son?"

"No, no, we didn't do that in those days. I'm glad they didn't, because I don't think I could have taken that." And he laughed again.

"How did you feel about it—when your son was born? I know, for a lot of people, that's an overwhelming experience."

He said with stoic pride, "It didn't overwhelm me."

"Did you ever take care of your son when he was a baby?"

He smiled. "I never changed his diapers one time."

"That's amazing," I commented. "Usually, fathers never completely escape it."

"That was in the olden days." Spies chuckled. "When that was considered women's work. You don't think I'm particularly too bad a fellow, do you?"

I grinned at him. "No. You're an academic—that's clear."

"I focused on my studies because I knew it was sink or swim. It was the most difficult work of my life, really."

"When you were doing your Ph.D."

Spies nodded. "Yes. I thought I had it difficult when I was an undergraduate at USD. But it was nothing compared to what I had when I was getting my Ph.D. That was the most trying time of my life. I used to become so tired that I'd wish that I could get sick so that I could get a chance to rest. That's really the truth."

"That sounds like it was grueling."

"It was grueling to no end," he responded.

"Who were your mentors or influences at this time?"

Spies said, "A man by the name of Nathan L. Drake, He was a Harvard—a Ph.D. from Harvard— who had also studied in Germany. He was a very famous chemist. He knew his science, and he was a man that...he was very hard, but he was fair. And that's the way he operated. He was very truthful, and so we got along quite well."

I began, "So he taught you —"

"Well, you didn't say, 'Will you teach me how to do research?' " Spies answered. "I learned it from what he said. I associated with him for a number of years. I worked right in his office, as a matter of fact. I had a little desk," he laughed, "an extremely small wooden desk. I couldn't even write on it because it had a rough, uneven surface."

"What do remember from those years with Drake?"

"One particular experiment stands out," Spies answered. I was taking a class from Professor Drake, in which we were learning about the identification of compounds. One day in class Professor Drake gave us an unknown, and we were supposed to identify it by chemical test. And I got on a substance, an aromatic ether, that I simply could not do. I knew what the substance was, but I didn't know how to prove what it was. I worked and worked on it for weeks. Finally, my roommate, who was also in chemistry, took pity and gave me a hint as to how to identify it by chemical means. Otherwise, I'd probably still be out there working on it." He chuckled, adding, "We also had to learn German and French to get the Ph.D. in chemistry."

"Why?"

Spies explained, "Because Germany was the center of science at that time, and France—they just threw that in. They were quite good scientists too. But I always said that I was more interested in doing things, so that the German boys would have to learn English in order to read my stuff, rather than the other way around."

He said that with a certain arrogance that was distinctly American.

I asked, "Did you then read the works of scientists who were German?"

"No," he answered, "I just became sufficiently proficient to pass the exams. And I never used it afterward." He paused, considering his words. He amended, "It would have been a little help, but not that much help. It was no handicap to me, really, not to read their stuff."

He continued, "As a graduate student in chemistry, I also was expected to give seminars. I had never had any public speaking. When I got up to speak the first time, I felt it must be obvious that I was shaking with fear.

"I decided that the best way to overcome this fear was to take on more speaking engagements, to just keep doing it until it became second nature. In preparation for each speech, I would write the first part of each sentence that I would use in the speech on a 3" x 5" card. Then, I got where I could memorize word for word a speech that would last forty-five minutes to an hour. It was not easy. I had to practice and practice. And I would do just great."

"You'd memorize your speech?"

"Yes, I'd memorize it," he answered. He was obviously very proud of his ability to do this.

I asked, "Did you ever get up in front of somebody and that speech would just go out the window?"

"It never did," Spies said. "No, I couldn't do that now—it'd go now." He laughed. "And I got so that I really sort of enjoyed speaking finally. But I just had to pound myself into it. That was the hardest thing—one of the hardest things I ever did was to learn to speak publicly. Eventually, I got so that I didn't need the cards. I used them in memorizing the speech ahead of time, and it wouldn't even bother me if they asked questions in the middle of my speech. I would simply pick up right where I had left off."

I said, "You mentioned earlier that Professor Drake was

your biggest influence. Did he steer you a certain direction?"

Spies paused, considering this question. "During this period, I learned what chemistry was all about. At South Dakota I learned the techniques of chemistry, but I didn't learn how to do research. At Maryland, as a graduate student, I did learn how to do research, which was a great thing for me."

"Were you publishing at this time?" I asked. "Were you starting to do so?"

He nodded. "I had about eleven publications when I left there."

I was impressed. "That you had published while you were in your Ph.D. program?"

"Yes, and after," he said. "For the year afterwards."

He frowned, obviously thinking hard. "One thing I want to say, when you get a Ph.D.—I expect it's true of almost all people who get their Ph.D. legitimately—it becomes an attitude. You have a great bulk of knowledge. When you are faced with a problem, you apply all of that knowledge to a solution. You come up with an idea. If you think the idea can be implemented, then you find a place to start in your research and you're off. From there, you'll run into all sorts of new leads. Eventually, you either get the solution or you don't. It's an attitude, sort of."

I nodded slowly. "I think you're right. It's interesting to hear you say that."

"It's true of life too," he said. "Many people don't realize that that's what it is, but that's what it is."

I think I knew what he meant. We all have Ph.D.'s in life, and we apply the bulk of our knowledge to problems that arise. And, "eventually, you get the solution or you don't."

Spies consulted his notes, then continued. "The title of my Ph.D. dissertation was, *The Nature of Crotin-Resin from Crotin Tiglium Linn.* The crotin plant grows in China and the East Indies. It contains the most potent fish poison ever known, and it also has some powerful vesican action—reacting on the skin—which made it very difficult to work with."

"What was your purpose in conducting research on this?"

"As a possible plant insecticide," he replied. "After I earned my Ph.D. in 1934, I stayed on in the same capacity, only now I was no longer going to school. I worked on a method of analysis that involved nicotine, which is a powerful poison when it's free. If you get a drop on your skin, it may kill you. I distilled large amounts of nicotine in the process of purifying it. If the equipment had blown up when I was distilling the nicotine, I could have killed all of the people in College Park."

He looked intently at me. "One point I want to make is that— if I say so myself—I became a fairly successful person in devising procedures where none existed before. I was a successful research person. I attribute a lot of this to my ability to— when I was on the farm one time—well, not one time—"

"On a farm in South Dakota?"

"Yes. I drove a pushbinder, which has six horses and cuts a twelve foot swathe. When you run machines like that, with horses and all, you sometimes end up a good distance from home—maybe a mile or so—and you have a tendency to break down now and then. I was always able to devise some temporary solution to the breakdown, so I wouldn't have to go back home. I attribute this ability to being a great help in research. I could evaluate the situation posed by a problem and bring it to a successful conclusion."

I observed, "It taught you how to devise."

Spies nodded. "Yes." He set down his notes and looked at me. "Do you think we should break for lunch?"

"Sounds good," I said. I was surprised to hear the workaholic Dr. Spies say this. But I was ready too. I needed a break from chemistry and the interview process to mull over what Spies had been telling me in the last few hours and to get a fresh perspective.

During my lunch break, I wandered around Dr. Spies' neighborhood. There were very few houses in the area—so he told me—when his was built in 1937. That was hard to imagine. This part of Arlington was as much a part of the city as any other part, in no way resembling a suburb. The houses and the apartment buildings, which were quite close together, looked very similar, with the popular red brick facade. The place was teeming with traffic. When I walked over to a nearby mall, I sat and watched people and realized how true it is when people call Washington, D.C. cosmopolitan. This Virginia mall, located approximately five miles from the Capitol, presented a busy, constant flow of ordinary business people, senior citizens, and mothers with small children—a decidedly colorful mixture of blacks, whites, Hispanics, and Asians. If there was any minority, it was white.

That got me to thinking about Dr. Spies having lived here for the past sixty years. I wondered how this place had affected his thinking and whether he considered himself a true Easterner now. Certainly, he had spent many more years in this part of the country.

I returned to his house to resume interviewing. I was twenty minutes earlier than we had agreed upon, and when he ushered me in, I could hear the TV blaring in the dining room. I realized I had interrupted Dr. Spies's daily dose of "The Young and the Restless." He politely turned off the TV, however, and sat down with me at the table, ready to resume.

Knowing what a careful scientist Dr. Spies is, I couldn't help feeling that he had allowed me to see him watching his daytime soap opera. But I brushed that thought aside and waited for him to begin again.

10

A Professional Life in Chemistry

"In September of 1936," Spies said, "I received an offer to head a chemistry section of a new study on allergens of agricultural products. My Ph.D. professor, Nathan Drake, advised me not to take the job because he thought it was too difficult a problem. I took the job anyway—so much for his advice."

Spies laughed. It was obvious that Dr. Spies would only follow his mentor's wishes up to a point.

I asked, "How did you know you should take the job—especially since you had Drake's advice not to?"

Spies considered the question for a moment. "From my standpoint, it was a challenge and a terrific opportunity. I certainly felt as if I had nothing to lose. If the job was too hard or if I couldn't solve the problems it presented, they would still pay me and I would, in all likelihood, still have a job."

That was certainly logical. Still, I couldn't help seeing that Dr. Spies was a gambler.

He continued, "I would be hired on as a P-4, which is professional, level four, and I would be paid $3800 a year—terrific money in those days.

"This is when I got into my real life's work. The research group was headed by Dr. Henry Stevens. Dr. E.J. Coulson was head of the immunology department. I was head of the chemical investigations. Dr. Harry S. Bernton was our medical man on the team. I was fortunate to have an excellent assistant—Dorris C. Chambers, who was a medical technician. She also learned quite easily how to do necessary chemical techniques, and we worked together for many years."

This non-chemistry major struggled to understand what he was saying. "You were working on...allergens?"

He nodded. "The objective of my work was to isolate chemically and immunologically and characterize allergens of agricultural products. And we started working on cottonseed as our first allergen, our first substance."

"What was your purpose in doing this?"

"There was a thing called the Bankhead Jones Project, something Congress had dreamed up. The Bankhead Jones deal was funding for projects that were sort of far out. You know what I mean?" He looked at me inquiringly. "They thought they ought to work on it."

"There were no immediate gains?" I asked.

"No," he said. "Most of my stuff was not immediate."

"So this particular project was long-term."

Spies nodded. "It was funded for five years. And we worked on it for about thirty-seven years." He chuckled, adding, "I know some people raised their eyebrows when I said that at a banquet out in South Dakota. They thought I should have been fired at the end of five years, I guess."

I observed, "It seems your research was so useful that you could continue."

"Well, somehow we did," he said, "although at times we did see in the newspaper that our project had been cut out—but still we survived." He laughed. "I was glad I could just concentrate on my work in the laboratory, because I couldn't stand all of the bickering and biting and political maneuvering that went on."

I could see that. Dr. Spies went about his job without much fuss. Independent, focused on his work.

He continued, "I was the the kind of person who liked to work alone. I didn't like to get in and be a head of a big organization. I liked to get down and dirty. I always needed a hands-on approach to the problems. That was the way I worked.

"Dr. Stevens was a good man to have in charge, because he was able to kowtow to the administrators, you know"—he laughed— "and I wouldn't have been able to do that."

I said, "He was able to network ..."

"Yes. He believed in applying...do you remember Carnegie's system?"

I wasn't sure what he meant. "The library?"

"No, no." Spies explained, "Carnegie, he was the man who had courses on how to get along with your boss."

Suddenly, it hit me what he meant. I grinned. "Oh—Dale Carnegie."

Spies chuckled. "Yeah, yeah. Dr. Stevens believed in that, and I didn't. Dr. Stevens had marvelous communication skills. I always felt that he could say 'good morning' with more effect than I could announce a Nobel prize-winning accomplishment in the laboratory." He laughed again.

I asked, "Did it make you impatient sometimes that you just couldn't deal with your work and had to worry about this political ..."

"Well, I didn't," he said. "He did that part."

So Dr. Spies got to avoid the networking process—which fit in with his anti-social, loner persona.

I asked, "When you first took this job, where were you living?"

"I had to drive to work from Riverdale, Maryland," he said. "That was convenient when I worked at the University, but not with this job in Washington, D.C. So I had a house built in Arlington, less than five miles from where I would be working. It was one of the first houses on the block."

"When did you move into it?"

He paused. "Let's see—we moved into it in July, 1937. It was very convenient. I didn't have to spent a lot of time traveling back and forth to my office."

"Where was your office?"

"In the south building at the Department of Agriculture."

"Would you come home at lunchtime?"

Spies shook his head. "Oh no. I brownbagged it."

I asked, "Did you have time to do any stuff with your family, now that you weren't in school?"

"Well, I was terrifically busy getting my career established ...but my wife and son and I would go on vacation for up to two weeks at the seashore. Later, we wouldn't have much time for vacations, and we did have a family of cats as well, that needed Renice's daily care and attention."

"Renice ran the household?"

He nodded. "I gave her a fixed amount of money that she could count on every month for household and family expenses."

"How about Carl?" I asked. "Did you spend much time with him?"

"As Carl got older, I played games with him like horseshoes, badminton, and chess. And I never let him win. It made him very determined to beat me at these games, which, eventually, he did. I think it made him a good tennis player in college later on. We also used to listen to a lot of radio programs together. When I would give Carl his two-dollar allowance every Friday, he would say, in imitation of the gangsters on one of the radio programs, 'Gimme my two clams! Gimme my two clams!'

"I decided to play a joke on Carl, and one Friday, when he demanded his 'two clams,' I put two actual clams in his outstretched hand. I had gone down to the waterfront and gotten them just for the occasion." Spies laughed.

"At that time, Carl didn't think it was very funny. Teenagers tend to lose their sense of humor when parents play a joke on them—especially if there's money involved. I did give him his allowance eventually."

I observed, "So you did manage to squeeze in time with both Renice and Carl—in between working at your new job."

Spies looked rueful. "It wasn't easy. My work was very demanding, right from the beginning."

"How did you start out?"

"When I first started the work for the Departmentof Agriculture," Spies said, "I had to equip a laboratory, starting from scratch. One of the first things I did was to install a microanalytical laboratory using the techniques that I had learned at the University of Maryland, which I used throughout my career." He added, as an afterthought, "The federal government, of course, paid for all of this equipment."

"Can you describe the technique you used in layman's terms?"

Spies paused. "Well, I can best say that...when, for example, you determine the carbon content of a substance you burn it. Maybe it'd best be described by saying it required only one one-thousandth of the amount formerly used by the older method. The work was done on milligram samples instead of gram samples."

"What was the advantage of using this method?"

Spies answered, "Being able to use such miniscule amounts to determine the structure of a substance was very important in research. In order to determine the structure of rotenone, for example, you'd sometimes end up with very small quantities of material, which, by the older methods, we would not have been able to analyze. With this new method, we could use a thousandth of the amount we used to have to use to do research.

"This method required a special balance for weighing. You had to have special equipment to get the sensitivity. It was fortunate that I was able to purchase exactly what I needed to do the work."

I asked, "You had learned this technique at the University of Maryland?"

Spies nodded. "Yes, I did the whole thing, started it. It wasn't my idea, but I did all the work. I used to go up there—

I remember working on New Year's Day because I was so interested in getting it underway and all." He laughed. "Worked on holidays and everything."

I commented, "You were extremely dedicated."

"Whenever I attacked a problem, it became the most important thing in my life at that moment, until I succeeded." He paused. "Now, contrary to what Mr. Nixon said about how you should never give up, sometimes in research you have to give up because you're unable to do the job. It doesn't necessarily mean it can't be done. There just turned out to be certain limitations, in which case, it would be foolish to work on a problem that was insolvable for the rest of my life." He paused, looking at me intently. "Do you know what I mean?"

"Yes." I did understand. His approach was so logical. I doubted whether I would have been able to give up working on something once I had gotten started, though, insolvable or not.

Spies concluded, "Like Kenny Rogers, I had to learn when to fold and when to hold—had to know when to drop the problem."

"How did your wife handle your dedication to your scientific pursuits?" I asked. "Working on New Year's Day and so on?"

He looked sheepish. "I'm sorry to say that she suffered from that."

"Did she get upset with you over this?"

"No, she was very patient," he replied. "And very understanding. And she had her cats." He chuckled, then consulted his notes again. "Now, in regard to testing of allergenic potency, you are trying to isolate something. You want to get the allergen free from all other products in the seed. There may be as many as fifty products or so that make up a seed. And these allergens require a very small amount to give a positive test."

I asked, "How would you separate out the allergen?"

"Well, that's technical." He hesitated. "I don't think we can go into that. It's just too prolonged and complicated."

"I'd need a chemistry degree, and so would the reader?"

"Yes." Spies chuckled, looking down at his notes. "The testing was done on human subjects at the Providence Hospital. And this was Old Providence Hospital in Washington. It was a Civil War hospital. This is where we did our first tests.

"Dr. Bernton had a clinic, an allergy clinic there. We selected patients that were of the proper sensitivity for making the test. And Dr. Bernton approved the tests—he was a medical doctor. A person like myself, with a Ph.D.—we could not work on humans without medical supervision. Although Dr. Bernton trusted me enough to let me devise any test I wanted, which I did, but he knew what they were and all."

I tried to see the big picture. "Somebody would come in with allergy problems of some sort, and he would find out what they were allergic to and if they were allergic to things you were interested in ..."

"Yes, yes."

"So they were guinea pigs in some sense."

"Sure," Spies said. "But the reason for having a medical man was to make sure that we didn't conduct any tests that would hurt people in any way."

Mindful of my own allergies, I asked, "Would your testing change or improve their allergy problem in any way?"

Spies answered, "Yes, in a general way, not specifically. Because, the more you know about an allergen, the better chance you have of coping with it, you know. But it wouldn't necessarily help them, except they got special treatment from us, by the methods that were already in vogue at the time.

"Our first paper was published in *The Journal of Allergy* in January, 1939.[1] In the paper, we explained that the sensitivity to CS 1 from cottonseed did not indicate sensitivity to cottonseed oil, citing as evidence the cases of four allergy patients, all of whom tested allergic to cottonseed but not to cottonseed oil.

"Now, one of the reasons that we got started with cottonseed— Dr. Stevens was interested in what happens to one of the Mayo Brothers, who thought he was sensitive to cottonseed oil."

Ah, the Mayo Brothers. I recognized the name because of the world-famous Mayo Clinic in Rochester, Minnesota.

Spies continued, "Consequently, wherever Dr. Mayo would go on his various speaking engagements, he would have to make sure there was no cottonseed oil in the preparation of his food. And our— one of our objectives was to determine that cottonseed oil and sensitivity to cottonseed itself were not the same thing. The oil, in other words, contained no allergen. And the allergen was present in the seed."

I asked, "So a person could be allergic to the seed itself, but not to the oil—because the allergen wouldn't be present in the oil?"

"As a matter of fact," Spies said, "we actually fed those people that were sensitive to cottonseed the oil in large quantities, and it had no effect on them."

"Now, why is that?"

Spies shrugged his shoulders. "It just is, that's all."

Puzzled, I asked, "So, Dr. Mayo was imagining that he had this allergy? Was he allergic to something else then?"

Spies explained, "He was probably allergic to the whole cottonseed, but not the oil itself. Possibly, the oil he used was not separated completely."

I said slowly, "So, if the oil's not separated properly, then he could have an allergic reaction."

Spies nodded. "Yeah, I don't think that's very likely, though." He consulted his notes again. "Our research had considerable economic importance in cottonseed sensitivity. We wrote a series of seven papers, describing our work in cottonseed allergens.

"We then turned to a study of the allergens in castor beans, and other allergens that were similar to to cottonseed were also isolated and studied. In other words, we used the same method that we used for isolating the allergens from cottonseed and applied them to other oil seeds. And castor beans turned out to be quite similar, although the allergen's different because it has a different specificity. Do you know what that means?"

When I shook my head, he responded, "It means the allergen in castor beans reacts only with people who are sensitive to castor beans, not to cottonseed. Is that clear?"

"Yes, it is."

Spies resumed his narrative. "In the meantime, Dr. Coulson was publishing a series of papers on the immugenic properties of allergens. Immunochemistry is the—I don't know where to start— an antigen is similar to an allergen, but there are differences. So you can't say they're exactly the same. If you inject a guinea pig with an antigen, it produces antibodies which react specifically only with that substance that you used to sensitize it with. Dr. Coulson had a large colony of guinea pigs which he used. He also used rabbits and rats for his study.

"He began publishing a series of papers on the immunochemistry of allergens, starting in 1940. These studies were on the allergens isolated by myself. The procedure worked out for cottonseed and castor beans was applied to other oil seeds. This resulted in new classes of substances which we called natural proteoses. The substances we studied were almond nuts, Brazil nuts, castor beans, cottonseed, filbert—filbert, flax seed—kapok seed, and mustard seed. This method is summarized in a chapter of a book entitled *Immunochemical Aspects of Foods*.

"Because it took many years to work out the method for studying the cottonseed, we just applied that same method to these other substances. Now, you see, you couldn't do this similar substance—this similar study, say, on mustard seed. It took many years to work out this method for cottonseed. So if we just applied that method we used to these other substances, this was a great step forward in terms of saving time and effort. As I stated in Chapter 15 of the book *Immunological Aspects of Foods*, "The importance of studying cottonseed allergens originally was intrinsic but later became prototypic when allergens of similar nature were isolated from other oilseeds by the same procedure developed for cottonseed."[2]

"In this same chapter, which was published in 1977, I looked back on the accomplishments of that time, setting our research in historical perspective: 'In the middle 1930s, the U.S. Department of Agriculture (USDA) became interested in allergens of agricultural products because reports of alleged sensitivity to edible cottonseed products were adversely influencing the cottonseed industry.'[3] At that time, I explained, allergists generally believed that 'allergic sensitivity to cottonseed denoted sensitivity to cottonseed oil.'[4] The research we conducted disproved this theory. I acknowledged that 'although more sophisticated techniques for studying allergens are now available, our conclusions are valid and therefore, of current as well as historical significance.'[5] I expressed the hope that this subject would be investigated further, because of world hunger—specifically, because of 'the increased need for proteins for human consumption.' "[6]

This did indeed seem like a noble long-term objective—research done for the purpose of ending world hunger—or, at least, decreasing it.

Spies continued, "For the work we had accomplished in the field of allergy, Dr. Stevens, Dr. Coulson, and I received the Hillebrand Prize in 1950, which is considered one of the highest honors in American chemistry. This was the first time the award had been shared by three recipients."

I wondered if this was the height of Dr. Spies' career. What he and his co-workers had accomplished was certainly most impressive.

Looking tired, Spies said, "Now, I don't know whether we should continue any longer today."

"Let's stop then," I said at once. I could see that talking about chemistry exhausted him. And he had given me a lot to mull over.

Dr. Spies and others like him, who are so dedicated to their work, while they make these significant advances in their fields, must sacrifice something in the process. In Dr. Spies' case, that appeared to his homelife, to a certain extent.

We resumed the interview the next day. We were discussing "unique" methods of research.

Allergens Investigation Team
U.S. Department of Agriculture, Washington, D.C. ca. 1960.
L. to r. Back row: Drs. Harry S. Bernton, Joseph Spies, Robert Williams, E.J. Coulson, William J. Stein. Front row: the project secretary, Dr. Henry Stevens, and Mrs. Mabelle Montgomery.

Spies said, "Back in the late 1950s and early 1960s, we were able to use prisoners for our research."

I raised my head at this. "Really? For what, specifically?"

"For studying allergens, for much of the work that we did."

"Why prisoners?"

Spies shrugged his shoulders. "Well, because they're available. They're as near to guinea pigs as you can get. You wouldn't be able to do that work now because of the legal ramifications of it."

I could certainly see that. But what Dr. Spies said next would send any legal department into a tizzy.

"Dr. Bernton was able to get free cigarettes from a tobacco company, which we used for payment. We gave those prisoners two packs of cigarettes per visit, which is all those fellows got for being guinea pigs for our research. Of course, they also got a break in their prison routine, which was important to them."

"So would you go to the prison?" I asked.

Spies nodded. "I kept a log of it. I made 347 trips to Occoquan, Virginia."

"So these prisoners were glad to get away from their routine."

"Yes, they were." He laughed. "And our tests began...this is a situation, again, where a medical doctor was necessary because we couldn't do anything without the presence of a doctor."

"You couldn't do any kind of tests on human beings without a doctor."

"That's right," he answered. "Nowadays, there's so much red tape that you couldn't do this work at all."

Yes, I suspect these sorts of experiments would now be viewed as treating prisoners as something in between humans and guinea pigs.

I asked, "Was this the only prison that you worked with?"

"It is the only prison I did. Dr Bernton did some work at Lorton Prison, which is where the hard-time penitentiary types were imprisoned, where people got held hostage sometimes. I didn't go up there."

"I don't think I would have either."

Spies chuckled. "Some prisoners had tattoos of naked women on their arms. And I would say, 'This is going to hurt her worse than it does me.' And I would plunge the needle into her buttocks—that is, into the tattoo on the prisoner's arm." He laughed again. "It was a test on his arm, but it was in a tattoo that was on this fella. Those fellows had a good sense of humor. They were nice to work with. They gave you a different point of view on things."

I tried not to show how shocked I was by this side of Dr. Spies. He could be pretty earthy for a scientist. I said only, "They were glad to get the cigarettes, I take it."

"Oh, yes," he said. "That was a medium of exchange. They used them for money. Yes, very glad." He laughed again.

"You mentioned earlier that you published eighty-five papers," I said. "What drove you to publish?"

"Oh, publishing is our life. That's how we get our recognition."

I observed, "That's such an enormous amount of publishing for anyone, really."

"It is," he agreed. "And, like I said earlier, I was a person who mostly liked to work alone—although I was able to work quite well with Mrs. Dorris Chambers. We worked together so wonderfully for so many years."

I smiled. "She was your right hand?"

"Yes, she certainly was. And so efficient. She worked with me—let's see—during the forties and into the fifties. Almost all through the fifties, I'm sure."

"What was her background or training?"

"She was a medical technician," he replied. "But she was able to pick up chemical techniques too. And that's how we got along. It was just terrific—I had complete confidence in her."

Lowering his voice, he said, "I believe Mrs. Chambers had had an illness once before she came there where she was bedridden for a year almost. I don't know what her trouble was."

"Do you remember what she looked like, what kind of personality she had?"

Spies paused. He was obviously not used to thinking of anyone in physical terms. "Well—she was a tall lady. She was not particularly good-looking. But she was a person that didn't mince words. She said what she meant and she meant what she said. She had a lot of common sense, in addition to great skill as a technician. And she was able to develop the techniques that I wanted, from a chemical standpoint. And she was of terrific use to me. I could just tell her something, tell her the method, and she'd work it out on her own."

"She was able to resolve problems by herself?"

"In a way," he said. "Oh, I'd forgotten this—she also kept up on the stock market and became quite an authority. She really understood it."

"So would she advise you?"

He nodded. "She did. I bought quite a few stocks, and I still have them, as a result of her advice."

Although Dr. Spies could make chauvanistic remarks at times—the story about the prisoner's tattoo comes to mind—he also showed respect for Dorris Chambers' intellect and respected her abilities obviously. In some ways, he was ahead of his time in his attitude toward women.

I said, "I'm curious—not to get off the subject, but—you mentioned the Bankhead Project funding for your work. The government was interested in this research—not for any specific purpose—but generally speaking, because it might be useful?"

"Yes," he said. "You never know what's going to come from this research. And while we did it, we of course naturally feel it's important enough to do, at least."

I asked, "And I imagine, even though you were dealing with a very specific type of research, it would lend itself to other types of research—the methods you would use?"

Spies nodded again. "I did a lot of collateral projects over the years as they came up. One time Mrs. Chambers and I spent years working on another subject. It was related—it came up because of this research, but it was not directly related to it.

"My work in allergen research allowed me great freedom of choice of activity. I wanted to use an existing method in my research, and I ended up making some modifications to an existing method because it was apparent that they needed modifying. One thing led to another, and Dorris Chambers and I ended up working on the determination of tryptophan for four years." He laughed, shaking his head. "In fact, we took time out from our work on the chemistry allergens to do this—that's how much freedom I had."

It sounded incredible—to have your talent, intellect, and dedication to a particular field recognized, to be allowed to pursue it as you saw fit. This, in essence, is what the government had given Dr. Spies the latitude to do.

I commented, "That sounds great. In the process, you developed a new method departing from this old method?"

Spies paused. "Well, our research during this period resulted in a series of papers. As a matter of fact, I fought with the reviewers of one of my tryptophan papers for an entire year.

"The Dept. of Agriculture had to review and approve everything that we were going to submit for publication. I argued with these peer reviewers to get four separate papers accepted for publication. The arguments went on endlessly. In the process, I got one reviewer disqualified. When it was all said and done, the four separate papers turned into one single paper—61 pages of single-spaced typing, as I recall.

"When they finally accepted that paper, I walked home slowly, feeling at peace with myself, satisfied with what I had managed to accomplish. That was one of the happiest moments of my life. That particular tryptophan paper eventually received a Citation of Classics in 1977.[7]

"What this organization does is to go through the literature in the field, and if the paper in question is cited, they mark that down. That's the way they keep track of the number of citations." He added for clarification, "I didn't do this."

I said, "They determined, because it had been cited so many times, that it was a citation classic."

"Yes, right. That made me feel pretty good."

I said, "Yeah, I can see why." So here was yet another high point in Dr. Spies' career.

Spies consulted his notes. "According to the *Science Citation Index*, from 1961 to 1975, the paper had a total of 739 citations in the literature, making it one of the most cited papers of all times. The paper, 'Chemical Determinations in Tryptophan in Proteins,' described a method for which there had been a considerable need." He looked at me earnestly. "I wouldn't say that it was that important from the overall standpoint of science, but it did describe a method that was needed very much and used a lot. That's why it was cited so many times.

"When I received this special recognition for the paper, I thanked them in a letter and went on to describe how the paper evolved, as well as the agony I went through in getting it published." [8]

He finished reading the letter and smiled at me. "When the tryptophan paper was first published in 1949, I would get— say— fifteen to twenty requests for reprints in a single day. It was really wonderful. That made me feel very good."

I observed, "That would be time-consuming, wouldn't it?"

"Oh, I wouldn't have to write a letter," he said. "I'd just have to send a reprint in most cases. Once, a man wrote, asking for a reprint of the tryptophan paper. In his letter he practically called me a know-nothing. He thought Mrs. Chambers was in charge of all of the work on the project. I should have had Mrs. Chambers answer his letter." He laughed. "But I just ignored it."

I said incredulously, "He wrote and asked for a reprint and insulted you at the same time? That certainly takes a lot of gall."

"Yeah," Spies replied, laughing. "It sure does."

He consulted his notes again. "In addition to my work on tryptophan, I published many papers that were offshoots of my regular work.

"For example, my work involved isolation of chemical characterization and clinical characterization of a new class of proteins classified as CS-1A-like complexes, CS-1A-like proteins, which was responsible for the principal allergenic activities of oil seeds such as castor beans. Then there was my work on milk allergies."

It was obvious from Dr. Spies' pause that he considered his research with milk allergies to be significant.

"About five years before my 'normal' retirement from the Dept. of Agriculture," he began, "I was told by the administration to stop working on oil seed allergens and work on milk allergies. At first I thought of retiring instead of starting this new project."

I could see Dr. Spies initially resisting being told to stop research on one subject and begin on another.

He continued, "Then I got to thinking about milk allergens. I had always had an idea that action of digestive proteins might produce antigens for allergens with a specificity different from that of the undigested protein. This seemed unlikely, but it would explain why native proteins do not give a positive skin reaction, where the person is clinically sensitive to the digestion of products. I had an idea that could be demonstrated with techniques available in our laboratory.

"The procedure was known as a Schultz-Dale procedure. I decided to have a go at it. And that was what stimulated me to study milk allergies instead of continuing—it really was a good idea because I think I had exhausted all I could do on oil-seed allergens."

I couldn't help wondering if Dr. Spies would have been able to admit that at the time.

He continued, "It is interesting that the work on demonstrating new antigens reached the point of failure. We had not been able to demonstrate the new antigens, and I went to the medical library at the National Institute of Health in Bethesda, Maryland one day to consider dropping the project or modifying it. But as dumb luck would have it...

"On that same day, my assistant Mary Ann Stevan, in a final test, showed by dialysis of pepsin digestion of products that the new antigens were demonstrable. This unlocked the key to the whole problem. With these key results, we were able to go forward and make progress on the study of milk allergy. We discovered that the new antigens are probably produced by two to four minutes of pepsin digestion. Pepsin," he added, "is the stomach enzyme which starts the breakdown of ingested foods."

He paused, obviously proud of this breakthrough. "A review of our work on milk allergy was published in *The Journal of Milk and Food Technology*. The scope of the work is outlined in the abstract of the paper."[9]

He proceeded to read the abstract.

When he finished, he set down the article and looked at me—with what I, the nonexpert, would describe as a "Mad Scientist" gleam in his eye. He said, "Pepsin is the first digestive enzyme that the food encounters when you ingest it. It's remarkable—in the time of two to four minutes you have the production of these new antigens.

"This work on milk allergy is cited a few times, but it has really been overlooked. I think it is extremely important. I think they really haven't discovered it."

Clearly, he felt strongly that further research needed to be done. I asked, "What about allergy clinics? Have they taken advantage of any of this research on milk allergies?"

Spies explained. "Eventually, they may consider our research and results, but not necessarily very strongly."

He looked at me then, something in his manner suddenly less formal. "What do you say we take a break? Do you drink coffee?"

I perked up at this. Coffee addict that I am, I was not used to going without coffee for long periods of time (hours). We went into Dr. Spies' kitchen.

I was pained to discover that what Dr. Spies called coffee was that instant stuff. Still, I thought grimly, it's better than nothing. He heated water on the stove and set out two cups. Carefully, he measured the coffee with a teaspoon. Apparently, this was something he didn't do all the time.

We stood looking out his kitchen window into the back yard, sipping our hot brew. I could see an empty fenced-in area—for his birds? But those questions I decided to leave for later.

Studying his uncompromising profile, I couldn't help thinking how he looked much younger than his ninety years—and then I was astonished, thinking how strange it would be to be reminiscing about one's life—looking back fifty, sixty years earlier. I guessed that we were nearing the end of Dr. Spies's narrative about his years as a chemist.

When we sat down at the dining room table again—a second cup of instant in hand—Spies, in his logical, organized way, picked up where he had left off.

"Near the end of my career, I wrote a review of past work, entitled 'Allergens,' which was published in *Agricultural and Food Chemistry*." He read the abstract for this work.[10]

Spies said, "I also was a member of numerous scientific organizations, attending numerous meetings and other functions." He handed a sheet of paper to me. "Here's a paragraph that tells my activities with respect to that."

I glanced through an extremely long list of scientific organizations of which he was a member. "Dr. Spies, when did you find time to do all of this?"

Spies laughed, pleased by the implied compliment in my question. "I don't know. As I look back, I really don't have the slightest idea how I was able to do this, but my interest never lagged in anything devoted to science."

I observed, "You must have had to attend numerous meetings."

"Oh, I did," he said. "Actually, they didn't take as much time as they might seem to have. Many of those organizations didn't take any of my time at all."

"In which ones do you feel you made your greatest impact, that you felt you made your greatest impression or contributions? Or that you were particularly proud to be in, out of all the organizations?"

He replied, "Well, the American Chemical Society of Washington. And the American Academy of Allergy. I became a fellow in that. Those were the two main things, although I contributed to all the others."

I said, "Tell me about the American Chemical Society."

"I have been a member for over fifty years," he said proudly. "Actually, I had my fiftieth year celebration"—he laughed—"quite a few years ago."

"What about your role in some of these organizations?" I asked. "Did you help shape what directions they took?"

Spies nodded slowly. "I was a member of what's called the Board of Managers at the American Chemical Society of Washington for a number of years. Then I became a Counselor, which is a step above the Board of Managers, with national implications. I did this for many years. Then, when I first ran for president of the Washington chapter, I was defeated."

He shook his head ruefully. "It rather astounded my friends, who were sure that I would win. I shrugged my shoulders and said to myself, 'Well, if you don't want me—okay—I'll get along without you.' " And he chuckled.

"The next year, I was out photographing in the Badlands of South Dakota for a week. And they wanted to nominate me to run for president again. They had to have my reply in while I was out in the Badlands." He laughed again. "I got back just before the deadline to give them my reply. And I ran, and I was elected then. Everything comes the hard way for me."

It seemed that way. I asked, "What year was that?"

"That was in '57," he said. "I was elected for the next year, '58."

"So what were your duties as president?"

Spies said, "Oh, I had to preside over ceremonies, meetings, and that sort of thing. I did take my wife Renice on a trip to New York, to a meeting of the American Chemical Society where Vice-President Barkley—do you remember him—I don't even remember who was president at the time. But any way, he was the vice-president, and he spoke at the meeting. And we stayed at the Waldorf Astoria. That was one good thing." He chuckled.

I looked down at my notes. "In the February '58 issue of *The Capitol Chemist*, you were quoted, in a "Message from the President," and you're actually asking people to contribute funds to some chemistry-related thing—"

"Oh, yes, yes." He nodded.

I continued, "You made this declaration—and I thought it was really interesting: 'Excessive material remuneration is not a principal characteristic of the chemist. An appreciable part of his compensation, like that of other scientists, teachers, and the like, is measured in less tangible terms such as the personal satisfactions of daily experiences and their sense of overall contributions of the enrichment of human knowledge.' "

"That's right," he said.

"Do you still agree with these statements?"

Spies nodded. "Yes, I do. That's what I lived by during

those days. I certainly wasn't making a lot of money. I was pretty well paid—very well paid, I thought. And I really have a terrific pension now. I didn't save money for money's sake. I rather did it for my accomplishments. That's what counted with me."

Obviously, money was less important to Spies than doing what he cared about—and money was important only in so far as its ability to help him do what he wanted to do.

I asked, "As far as awards go, what stands out in your mind, that you're particularly proud of having received?"

"As I mentioned in that article—" he picked it up and read: 'the recognition of which Dr. Spies is proudest was the determination of the Scientific Institute for Information that according to *Science Citation Index*, his paper entitled "Chemical Determination of Tryptophane in Proteins" was cited' [11]— that's the one that gives me the greatest pride.

"And while it was very nice that I was co-winner of the Hillerbrand Award of the Chemical Society of Washington in 1950—sharing honors with Dr. Stevens and Dr. Coulson—triple awardees—I didn't value that award as much as I did the recognition for having one of the most cited papers. That has given me the greatest amount of pride. It's something not very many people have happen to them."

Perhaps Dr. Spies didn't value the Hillerbrand Award as much because it wasn't for something that was all his accomplishment. The cited article was clearly his brainchild.

I said, "That citation recognition clearly says how important your work was. You evidently influenced many people. I was wondering—did you influence your own son this direction at all?"

Spies smiled. "At one point, when my son Carl went to school at William and Mary, I went down there with him. And I was interested, of course, as a lot of fathers would be, in having him follow in my footsteps—become a chemist. And he started taking chemistry, but he soon found that he didn't have same love of chemistry that I did. He always joked that he would take half of the period for his chemistry class to set things up and

Dr. George W. Irving presenting Spies a plaque on completion of his presidency of the Chemical Society of Washington, 1959.

the other half to take things down, never actually getting anywhere. He soon got out of it, switching to psychology instead. He got a Ph.D. in psychology at Washington University in St. Louis and later taught at Kent State University."

"That is a completely different route he took," I said. I couldn't help thinking that it would very hard to follow in his father's footsteps in chemistry.

Spies said, "The thing about psychology or the social sciences—so-called—they don't have any solution ...any single solution. In chemistry, you have one solution. For the most part. There's always one answer. And that appealed to me more than anything else."

"That's an interesting distinction. Chemistry, in that way, is similar to mathematics."

He nodded. "Yeah, absolutely."

I smiled mischievously. "Of course, literature falls into that nebulous area."

Spies said hastily, "I don't run down those things personally—anything that appeals to you and you have a passion for is all right."

"Sometimes, when I'm teaching literature, I'd wish there was a single concrete answer."

We both laughed. I said, "Now—when did you actually retire from your job?"

"I retired officially from the Department of Agriculture in 1973," he replied. "It was mandatory that we retire at age seventy." His voice hardened. "Actually, they had decided to close down the project we had been working on when I was in my sixty-ninth year. I still had another year to complete, and, because of my seniority, I would be able to replace almost anybody. I told myself, 'I'm not really going to take another job. I'll just see what this seniority amounts to.'

"Do you know that they would not tell me where I would be assigned or what I would be doing? They wouldn't tell me a thing about it. So I played along with them for quite a while." He added, "Of course, I didn't want to make the people in personnel mad, because if you do that, they can make your life sheer hell from then on."

"Just with red tape?"

Spies nodded. "I had a friend who did that, who crossed the personnel people, and they certainly tortured him. Eventually, of course, I did officially retire. But I persuaded the Department to give me a place to work because I had a scientific publication to complete. Also during that time—in March, I believe—I agreed to do the chapter for the book on the oilseed allergen. It was very convenient to have those facilities available to me, because I knew that if I didn't do it while I had all equipment and research there, I never would.

"They gave a limited number of months in that office— three or four months, I think, to get the work done, and then I was supposed to get out of this place. But when the time came for me to leave, I just ignored that deadline. I stayed on until I got the work done. And I also got kind of mad at them.

"You're supposed to go through the official channels when you publish something from the Department of Agriculture. I ignored this and sent the article in without going through them.

I just published it on my own. This did not sit very well with the people in authority, but they got over it."

It was easy to picture Dr. Spies ignoring their rules and deadlines. He was, if nothing else, a get-things-done man who had no tolerance for the maddeningly slow, dull machinations of bureaucracy.

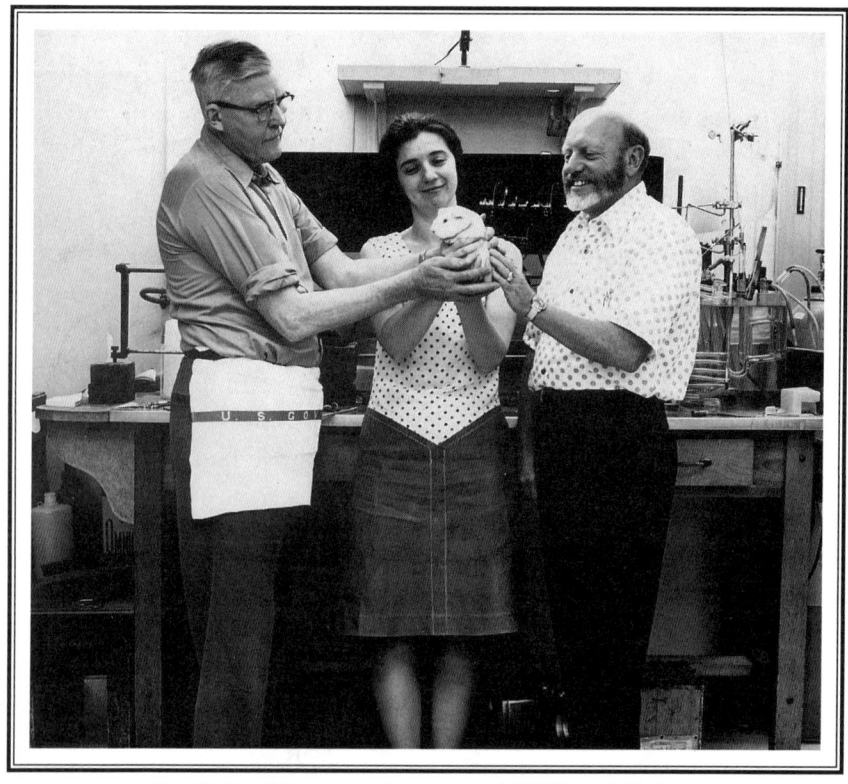

Joe Spies, Mary Ann Stevan, and William J. Stein
with the last guinea pig after closing the laboratory

11

The Chemist Photographs Cats

I asked, "Were you at all interested in photography as a boy?"

Spies nodded. "Yes. My sister Helen gave me a box camera for Christmas one year. I learned to take pictures and develop film with a candle and a red screen as the safe light. So I started taking pictures very early. I was a child almost. I don't know why I was so interested in taking pictures."

I glanced at my notes. "I remember reading you got a camera for Christmas at age fifteen, but you evidently had one before that?"

Spies nodded. "It was an Eastman Kodak, a Brownie." He paused. "This doesn't seem to jive quite because I thought that I got the camera later. It must have been another camera, but I don't remember that very clearly."

I asked, "When did you start to develop a love for animals?"

"Since my days at the I.O.O.F. Home, when I came under the influence of the writings of Thornton W. Burgess, I had a growing feeling of love and respect toward animals," he said. "My wife loved cats, and we had a whole family of them—as

Mrs. Renice Spies, ca. 1960

many as thirteen at one point, directly descended from a pair of cats a neighbor bestowed on us back in 1937, when we were first settling into our new home."

"Why did you photograph cats?" I asked. "Because you had already had them as pets in your home?"

He replied, "I took photographs of cats for several reasons. First, they are very photogenic. They have such beautiful and expressive eyes. Second... I came to regard photographing cats as a recreational hobby. The cats' activities were very amusing and restful. I had many belly laughs from observing their antics." He smiled. "They're really so funny. I simply loved the little animals for their own sakes, as individuals. Also, I preferred animals in general, rather than people, because—" he laughed— "because animals don't complain about the picture."

"That's the response you got from people?"

"Many times," he said. "Cats, on the other hand, never complain."

We both laughed.

Spies added, "I used to say that many times. I was sort of joking, and yet there was some element of truth to it also."

"Well then," I said, "I see why you chose cats. What attracted you to photography?"

Spies paused, considering this question. "Photography, generally speaking, gave me a chance to be competitive. I could submit my photographs in various contests. I loved competition." He shook his head. "Even so, at one point, I was ready to give up on winning any prizes or getting anywhere with my photography.

"I submitted my cat pictures to the International Amateur Snapshot Contest, which was sponsored by the *Washington Star* newspaper and the Eastman Kodak Company. I tried this contest for many years, never winning a prize of any kind.

"It's so typical of what has gone on in my life—that I had won nothing in the contests I submitted to for several years, and I had actually decided to stop sending in photographs. I was ready to give up, ready to admit that I just didn't have it in photography.

"There was about a five-to-six-week delay between the time you would send a photo in and you would hear from the publisher. During this time, I had decided not to send in any more photographs. Then I heard that a photograph I had submitted in the Star Contest had been accepted and was going to be published in their Sunday magazine.

"I won a $5 prize in the animals category for a photograph of a cat peering around a doorway. When it was published in *The Washington Star Sunday Pictorial Magazine* in 1951, I received fan letters from people, and I was almost as thrilled as I was when my first scientific paper was published.

Spies' first prize-winning photo.

"That photograph was taken with a $6.75 reflex camera, hand-held, using one flashbulb. To this day, out of the thousands of photographs I've taken, it remains one of my favorites.

"Greatly encouraged by this recognition from *The Washington Star*, I purchased an Eastman Kodak camera that was a little better quality than the one I had. Eventually, I also bought a Rolleiflex, which was a pretty good camera in those days."

"A Rolleiflex," I repeated. "What's the difference between a Rolleiflex and a 35 mm camera?"

Spies explained, "It's 120 size. Two and a quarter size. A Rolleiflex takes photos that are 120 mm, much better than what a 35 mm camera could do.

"I started taking pictures with the Rolleiflex, using a flash. I also built a dark room in my basement, so I could work at home developing prints. And, of course, I continued to send in pictures to contests.

"The next year I won the grand prize for that category. Because it was the grand prize, my picture was then submitted to Eastman Kodak's international contest. The grand prize, with respect to *The Washington Star*, meant that my photo was the best in ten weeks of competition with other photos that had been submitted during that time. So then I thought I really had it made when I did that. It encouraged me to take more and more photos.

"Eventually, I got the idea of doing a book on cats—my own cats, specifically. I felt so strongly that I knew cats and understood them and was able to portray what cats were like in photographs that I refused to look at any other book of cat photographs until I had published my own book first."

"Why is that?" I asked.

He replied, "Because I didn't want to be influenced by the interpretations that other photographers gave."

That made perfect sense. Dr. Spies, ever the maverick, was not one to imitate others.

He continued, "I worked every Saturday, Sunday, and holiday except Christmas for a whole year getting the pictures ready."

"You were able to work out of your home mostly, right?"

Spies nodded. "I did all of my own black and white work in my basement darkroom. My wife thought that I spent too much time on photographing cats. She thought I ought to wait until I retired. But you have to do that stuff when you're moved to do it. You can't wait until you're retired because it will never be accomplished if you do that."

Between cat photography and chemistry, I could see how his wife might have been exasperated occasionally.

I asked, "Did you ever get frustrated by the cats—you know—trying to get a certain type of photo?"

He shook his head. "No—although many people become frustrated trying to photograph cats. They complain that cats are too aloof and independent, that it's impossible to get past this barrier when photographing them.

"I always got what I wanted eventually. I had a lot of patience. I couldn't say, 'Now, cat, I want to take your picture. You get down there and pose.' What you have to do is make a game out of it that the cat thinks is solely for its benefit. Then you have your camera set up so you can snap the picture at a second's notice. If you set it up right, you can get the cat to perform for you. Make the cat think it's entirely for their benefit; that's the way you can get a good picture of a cat. You must have your camera ready and set up to take the picture. You must also have them perform in a place where they'll be in focus when you take the picture."

"That's pretty tricky, to get it all working together, isn't it?"

"No, it's not really—but it's necessary." He chuckled.

I consulted my notes. "I've got a quote here: October 27, 1958 issue of *Chemical and Engineering News*. You're quoted in regard to photographing cats. 'The secret is to turn the thing into a game which the cat regards as solely for their benefit,' which is an echo of what you just said. Would you say there is a playful side to your nature?"

"To my nature?" He seemed surprised by this question.

"Yes."

"Well, yes, there is. Like I said, sometimes, observing the cats' antics, I just had to break down and—you know, people would think I was insane." He laughed again.

I said, "The cats that you photographed—did they differ a lot? Did some sit very well, quietly?"

"They do vary a lot," he replied. "The best way you can photograph them is to select your own cats to photograph, and do it in your own home, in surroundings that are familiar to the cat."

"Do you think that people have misconceptions about cats?" I added, "The people I know who hate cats see them as very arrogant and selfish, not affectionate or loyal to people."

He said, "Well, I don't see cats as that at all. Cats have their own independence, and you take that into account in handling them. You don't try to make a cat into a dog. You change your personality into that of the cat rather than the other way around."

I glanced down at my notes again. "You judged a cat photography contest, I believe, called the Catography Trophy Competition, in 1967. You wrote a note indicating that you judged the photos, depicting cat personality first, technical quality second, handling of background third. My question, which you in degrees have answered already—I'll put it to you anyway—how does a good photographer go about bringing out the cat's personality?"

Spies replied, "You take the picture when the cat is at the peak of his activity. You know, a cat becomes very energized when he's playing or looking as if—he's keeping his eye on a toy mouse. They become intensely alive, so to speak. And that's when you have to take the picture."

"Because all of their energy goes into what they are doing?"

Spies nodded. "Yes. Now, with my cat photography studio, I used that at my home too. You know that picture, in which it appears as if the cat is charging? Actually, the cat is only stretching and yawning. How I took that—I used the cat photography studio that I had developed for taking pictures of purebreds. My technique was to pick up one of our cats when they were

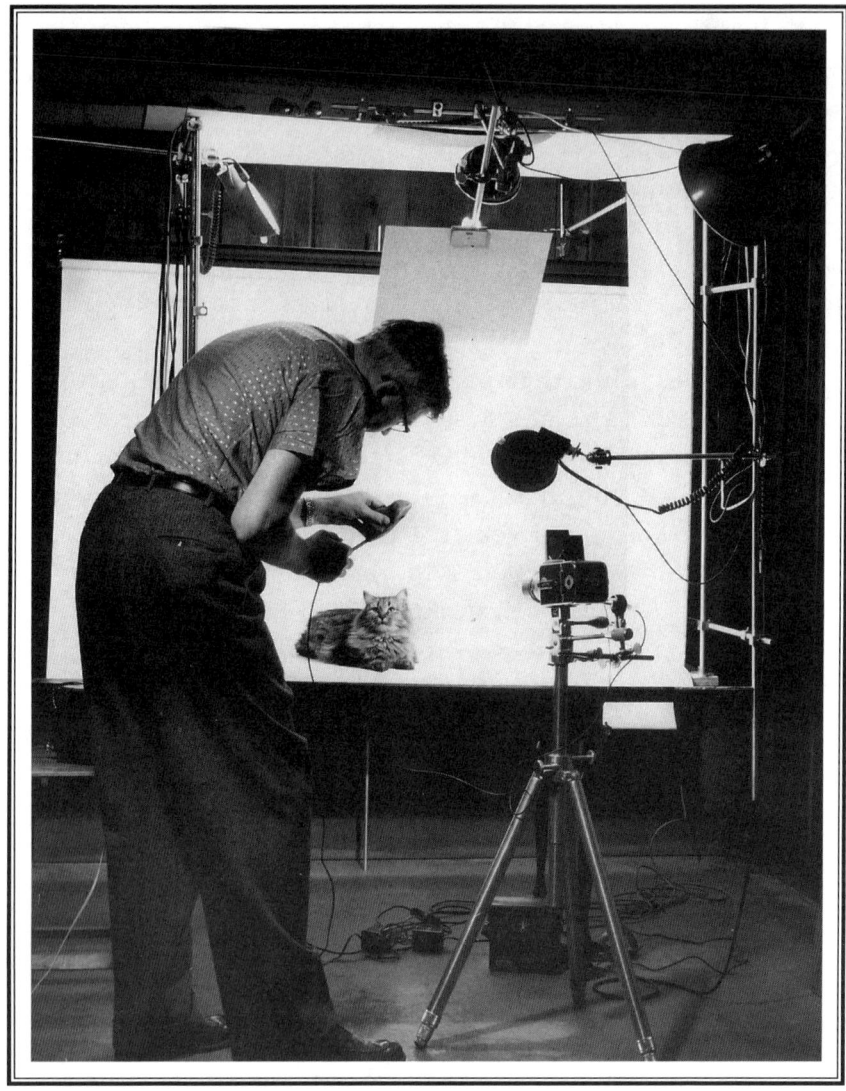

Spies and Portable Cat Photography Studio

sleeping and set them where they would be in the frame of the camera—in that apparatus—so they would be in focus. Our cats were used to being handled all of the time, so they didn't pay any attention when we picked them up and moved them while they were sleeping."

I commented, "I was wondering how you managed that."

"I'd sit there, watching television out of one eye; watching the cat out of the other," Spies said. "When the cat woke up, she'd stretch and yawn. And that's when I would take the picture."

"So she was actually in a pretty lethargic state in the picture?"

Spies smiled. "Oh yes." He held up a photograph. "Now, here's one picture I took, which I call 'Baker's Dozen' (see photo section) It won a prize. That picture was taken using a modification of this apparatus. I managed to get a good, in-focus, close-up shot of thirteen kittens, all sitting in a row."

I was astounded. "How did you do it?"

"I took the picture when they were waking up from a nap, of course," Spies said smugly. "If I had taken these cats and put them in front of the camera when they were playing, I never would have gotten the picture taken—never, never, never in the world. As they were waking up, I got their attention by lowering a board in front of the cats. And say, squeak a rubber mouse. They all looked at me, and I snapped the picture."

It was a great picture—all these kitten in a row, some of them cockily twisting their heads to follow the motion of a board or a rubber mouse.

"On another occasion," Spies said, "I took two sleeping cats and put them in this doll-size antique bed that I got from Renice's parents. I simply put the cats in the bed next to an alarm clock and waited for them to wake up before I started snapping pictures. That's how I achieved another prize winner, 'Time to Get Up' (see photo section) which won a grand prize in the Eastman Kodak contest, along with publication in *The Washington Star*.

"The bane of my existence was waiting patiently for the cats to wake up—sometimes a half hour or an hour—and having a visitor knock on the door." He sounded peeved. "Then the cat would wake up abruptly and walk away. I would have nothing to show for all of my troubles."

I understood. The scientist had been interrupted while conducting an experiment in cat photography.

Silhouette composite that appeared on the cover of *Cats Magazine*.

Spies continued, "When I photographed my cats, they eventually became like a part of myself. I got to know them so well that, when I would manipulate them, I felt as if they were almost an extension of my arm.

"For one photograph, I used about 25 sheets of printing paper when I was just starting out, to get the shadows right. Photography demands that you be not only patient but a perfectionist as well.

"For one particular set of silhouettes, it took me an hour and a half to expose the picture for printing. I had to get each silhouette separate and lined up and in proper proportion to the others. And I spoiled two of them in the process. So I just kept trying, until I finally got it right the third time around. The resulting photograph ended up on the cover of *Cats Magazine*."

I looked through a pile of photographs, many of them backyard shots of squirrels, birds, and raccoons. "It's amazing that you were able to get so many good nature shots in your backyard, in the middle of a city."

He looked pleased. "I feel that I got my best pictures in my back yard—don't you?"

"From what I've seen, I would say yes," I said. "It is incredible to me that you traveled all over the world, getting all kinds of photos of all these exotic animals. And at the same time, you spent days on end in your own backyard photographing fairly ordinary animals."

Spies nodded enthusiastically. "I got excellent shots of possums, raccoons, squirrels, and all kinds of birds in my back yard, right in the middle of Arlington, in an urban neighborhood, only five miles from the White House.

"These rather ordinary animals in my back yard had to compete with exotic animals from around the world, and they came out ahead."

"Why do you think these photographs were better?"

"Part of that had to do with my camera equipment setup in my back yard," Spies answered. "It is a big advantage to photograph from your own house. You've got all your equipment right there, and you can set it up whenever you want to, however you want to do it.

"I used to divide my life into five-year segments, in which I would try to master the challenge I had set for myself in photography, whether it was photographing mocking birds dive-bombing cats or blue jays or something else. I worked doggedly at photographing these backyard animals, pursuing it just as I did with photographing zoo animals or show cats or my own household cats.

"I would regularly set out peanuts and other food in the yard. As a result, I had everything from birds and squirrels to possums and raccoons showing up for dinner. On one occasion, I even saw a gray fox. The raccoons, possums, and foxes came at night."

He picked a photo from the pile. "Here is the set-up I used."

I glanced at this photo of a rather elaborate setup. "This is what you had in your backyard?"

Spies nodded. "If you were to go out into the yard and try to take a picture of a bird, you'd never get anywhere. What I did was concentrate all the action in one spot by attaching a bowl of dry roasted peanuts to the top of a post. My camera and electronic flashes were set up a few feet away. The electronic flash located up high would work at the speed of about one thousandth of a second, which would stop the action of the birds, even in flight.

"Since the distance was fixed, the shot would always be in focus. I used a 150 mm. lens on my Hassenblad, which is equivalent to a 100 mm. lens in a 35 mm. system."

I asked, "What was the device that you used so you could just take the picture from in here?" I gestured towards the kitchen. "You had a wire that ran outside?"

"Yes," he replied. "The camera would be tripped electrically with a long cable shutter release which ran into my kitchen.

"The background for the photos was set back about two and a half feet away, so I wouldn't get any shadow in the picture."

"So just setting it back far enough helps."

"Yes. The shadow was actually below the range of the camera eye," he said. "My backgrounds consisted of curtains on rollers, and I'd change the curtain color whenever I wanted to.

"I stayed inside, watching intently from the kitchen window. And when the moment was right, I would press the button on my remote wire and take a picture. I didn't have to be outside, pointing my camera and frightening the animals away. I took thousands of pictures that way."

We looked at several backyard photos together. I was very impressed by the camera set-up, his patience, and his talent in snapping these photos.

"These are great!" I said at last. I looked closely at a photo of a blue jay landing on the post. "For most people, that bird would be a huge blur—if they took that photo."

Spies laughed. "Admittedly, this process required a great deal of patience. I would sometimes sit at the window for several hours—before I would get the picture I wanted.

"Initially, this process required a few weeks for the wild birds to get used to the set-up and use the peanut bowl unafraid. Once they got over their fears, they came in droves.

"One of the best times to photograph birds is early on cold winter mornings when they are especially hungry—although activity continues throughout the day as a rule. Raccoons and possums come out to eat at night. Surprisingly, I could take photographs of them with a flash without scaring them away. Squirrels were active most any time during the day.

"I discovered it was considerably more difficult to get two blue jays in a picture than it was one. Photographing one blue jay had been comparatively simple. I then took on the challenge of getting three blue jays in the picture, and was only satisfied with the resulting photograph, after I had taken hundreds, if not thousands of blue jay pictures over a five-year span.

"The best photograph I ever took was of a squirrel surprising a blue-jay in the peanut bowl (sec photo section). Of course, there is some luck involved. You don't know that you've taken that kind of picture until you develop your film. This particular photograph ended up on the back cover of *National Geographic World*, a children's magazine. In addition, it was published, of all places, in *The National Enquirer*."

"What kind of film did you use to take these pictures?"

"For this kitchen-window photography, I only used 120 film," he replied. "In other words, there were only twelve exposures to a roll, which meant that, once I had taken twelve pictures, I would need to go outside and reload. It wasn't really a hardship, though, as I was usually ready for a stretch about that time.

"It was amazing how well all the different animals got along. One time a mother squirrel was killed and her two babies fell down in the chimney."

"In your house?"

"Yes," he said. "They stayed down there for two weeks before I could get them out. The two squirrels stayed around here and even became friends with the cats. I took a number of photos of these two little squirrels and the cats together, including one entitled, 'Friends.'

"One winter evening I came home and discovered a possum within twelve feet of my back-kitchen door. I let my cats out, and they followed him up a tree to investigate this strange little animal. They didn't harm him, and he didn't appear to feel threatened. He didn't bother to play 'possum.'"

My tourist instinct surfacing, I asked, "Did you take photos of some the famous sights around here?"

Spies nodded. "I took many photographs of nearby historic monuments and sites ... Mount Vernon, the Pentagon, the Arlington Memorial Amphitheater, the Jefferson Memorial, the Washington Monument, the Grant Memorial, Harpers Ferry, and the Arlington Cemetery. Many of these photographs appeared in various issues of *The Capital Chemist* during the late fifties and early sixties. People who knew me as a chemist were often very surprised to learn that I also did photography. Publishing in *The Capital Chemist* was one of the few ways I could actually combine chemistry with photography.

"As a matter of fact"—he consulted his notes—"the editor

for the January '57 issue of *The Capitol Chemist* added a humorous note to his editorial, saying, 'We don't deserve much credit for finding Joe's pictures, since he works just around the corner from us. All we need do is walk down the hall and yell, "Hey, Joe! Taken anything new lately?"' Spies chuckled.

"That would be convenient."

He continued, "I also take some photographs of natural scenery, such as the one entitled, 'Maelstrom,' taken at the height of the flood caused by Hurricane Diane in 1955. This particular photograph was not easy to get.

"I visited the scene of the flood on the night of August 20. Although Great Falls has a 76-foot drop, the gorge was completed filled with these angry waters, with no sign of a falls visible at all. I was so impressed by the spectacle that I got up early the next morning before dawn to photograph it.

"I exposed forty-eight frames in two-and-a-half hours. My photograph entitled, 'Maelstrom,' taken during this venture, was a runner-up in *The Washington Star*'s snapshot contest. I later learned that this flood, up to that point in time, was the fourth highest in Potomac history.

"Ironically, in August '57—just a few years later—I snapped some pictures of the Potomac River at one of the lowest stages in its history, from the same location I took the flood pictures. One of these low-water-level pictures appeared..." he checked his notes again "...in the February '58 issue of *The Capital Chemist*."

I said, "You also used an unusual photo-making process to create the birds vs. cats spoof—you know the one that I mean—that got published in *The Washington Post* magazine called *The Potomac*, *The National Observer*, and National Geographic's *Song and Garden Birds of North America* (see photo section). There was also a photograph called "The Hills Have Eyes" (see photo section) in which you set a huge pair of cat's eyes into a Badlands background. One cat magazine editor called it surrealistic."

He grinned. "A few critics said they always suspected that I was partially nuts anyway."

"Why did you do these kind of fantasy shots?" I asked. "Why didn't you just stick with purely realistic shots?"

He said, "My answer is: imagination. You know, imagination is the motivating force for scientific research, for any activity that you engage in. Your imagination conjures up things that you want to do. Then you have to devise techniques for fulfilling the ideas your imagination dreams up. I call those fantasy photos an exercise in imagination."

"So you just let your imagination take you where it would?"

Spies nodded. "And I had these pictures. When I took those photographs in the Badlands, I had no idea at the time that I would later be making fantasy photos from them. Somehow or another, I got the idea for doing it, and then, one thing led to another, and I came up with all of these."

I picked up the pictures and examined them carefully. "There's a very different feeling to those pictures."

Spies said, "Yes, well, they are mood pictures. And they're really sort of—they're obviously fantasies."

"Cat fantasies," I commented.

Spies laughed. "Yes."

I glanced at another photo. "It looks like you enlarged and cropped this photo."

"Oh yes, I took different parts," he replied. "When I first started doing photography, I was so dumb that I thought it was unethical if you cropped the picture in any way or if you didn't use the whole frame. Isn't that amazing? I learned differently along the way. And finally, I got to the point where I was using parts of one picture with another and all that sort of thing. The picture became the thing rather than how it was made."

"So your concept of what you thought a photo should be changed drastically."

Spies said, "Oh yes. In one of my Halloween photographs, I have a cat sitting on the roof of a house, howling at the moon (see phto section). It's actually three separate pictures, put together: a shot of the cat, a shot of the moon, and a shot of the roof of my house. I created many composite photos in this manner, sometimes using nine different shots to get the fantasy picture I wanted.

"Background or the absence of background in a photograph can be very important. That is especially evident in my book, *Big Cats and Other Animals*, in which I have almost eliminated from all of the pictures any evidence of the zoo where I actually took the pictures. Many people have assumed those photographs were taken in the wild."

He paused. "My wife's Alzheimer's was one of the reasons I took to photographing animals at the zoo. I don't know whether you've had any experience with it or not."

I shook my head. "Alzheimer's Disease? No, not really."

"When I started photographing animals at the Washington zoo, I needed a temporary form of escape. My wife had been diagnosed with Alzheimer's Disease. I took care of her. It can drive—the person who has it, I guess, suffers the most, of course, although, toward the end, I doubt whether most of them know something is wrong with them.

"I went out to the zoo three or four times a week to take pictures because it helped me keep my sanity. I think, if I had just stayed at the house with Renice all the time without doing anything but taking care of her, it really would have gotten to me. Fortunately, she could be left alone for short periods of time.

"I'd go as early in the morning as I could. When they would be open. And I'd stay two or three or four hours taking pictures. And then come back. I couldn't leave her alone any longer than that. I couldn't leave her overnight or anything like that."

I asked, "Did you cook the meals, or was she able to do some of that?"

"No, she was able to cook for most of the time—well, until I put her in the hospital."

"Was she able to keep house?"

"Sort of," he said. "Toward the end of her illness, she would start to scream at the top of her voice. And things like that. I'd jump up and put the windows down. I was afraid people would think I was beating her up." He chuckled. "Or something.

"When I'd go out in the evening, I did get the neighbors across the street to come over and act as babysitters for her, and all that sort of thing. Finally, she got where she had spells at night. I had to call the rescue people a few times, and they took her to the hospital. And the second time I did that, she didn't even know that she'd been to the hospital. I mean, that's the way they get."

I commented, "That must have been frustrating."

"It was," he said. "Scary too."

"Did she believe you when you'd tell her that you had taken her to the hospital?"

Spies nodded. "Yes, she did."

"She understood the nature of her disease?"

"Sort of," He said. "Finally—I was unable to give her the kind of care she needed, and I had to put her in a nursing home. She was there for about fourteen months. And while she was there, I agreed to revise my second book, *The Compleat Cat*. I worked on that project while she was in the nursing home. It got so bad, that when my son Carl was coming to visit her, I'd have to tell Renice a day ahead of time who was coming, explaining who he was and all. It was truly terrible. It drives a person crazy to try to—think."

I said sympathetically, "That was good that, all those years, you managed to cope. A lot of people wouldn't have been able to do so."

"Oh, I know," he said. "I just felt I owed it to her, after all those years she'd been so faithful to me.

"It's rather interesting," Spies added. "I used to go down to the nursing home every morning to see my wife. I went in the morning because it was—less cluttered. This one morning, I pulled up to the first stop sign near my house, and my car stopped. It wouldn't start up again. I had to take it to a garage for repairs and leave it. So I was not able to go down there that day. That same day, in the afternoon, my wife died. Isn't that strange that this would happen with my car on the day she died?"

"Yes." I agreed.

He looked out the front window. "I thought of that many times."

"How long did she have Alzheimers?"

"Well, it's hard to tell when it starts because it's so gradual. But she had had it for at least ten years. She had it progressively getting worse from 1973 on. And then—she died in 1984."

Dr. Spies was quiet. After a minute, I said, "I wondered what sort of person your wife was."

"Well—let's see." He looked at picture of a woman at the foot of the stairs in a government building. "There she is—wouldn't you know it." He laughed softly. "That's an exhibition at the Smithsonian Institute of my pictures. She was a person who...I guess what you're wondering about...if she had a life of her own. She was a secretary, and a darned good one. But after we got married, she devoted her life to raising our child and furthering my ambitions. She never worked outside the home."

This sounded insensitive but I could think of no other way to phrase it. "I'm wondering, why you married her out of all the various women you could have married."

"I just fell in love with her—that's all." He laughed again, this time a bit uncomfortable at his admission.

I said encouragingly, "Because she was a kind person, because she was—?"

Spies said, "She was kind and she had a good sense of humor—at least before we got married." He laughed heartily. "Probably diminished that."

I grinned. "I've heard marriage does that sometimes."

"Yeah." He looked at the picture again. "She doesn't look browbeaten, does she?"

"No, not at all," I said. "She looks happy to be there, and she's enjoying herself. What do you consider to be some of the most significant moments of your marriage?"

He paused, thinking. "Well, her loyalty, I guess, was one of the things that I prized most. I prized her loyalty above all.

There aren't many women nowadays who would tolerate what she had to put up with."

"It's a different era."

"Oh, entirely," he responded. "And I don't think it was all that bad. She never had to work. I won't tell you that she didn't eventually become kind of dissatisfied with me for running around so much, but, for the most part, she took pleasure in my accomplishments. She lived vicariously that way. Eventually she did think enough was enough. But we—we still stayed together."

I said, "So, Renice didn't have to work out of the home. I assume she ran the household."

"The way we worked that out," Spies explained, "I gave her a fixed amount that she could count on every month, and that's the way we got along. She handled her own money. It was her money, and I never touched that. And she managed all that."

I said, puzzled, "What do you mean by her own money?"

"She had things called ground rents in Baltimore, which was a good investment. They don't own the land there. At least it used to be that way. Their houses are built on the ground they rent."

"I've never heard of that."

"It's very rare," he said. "And those were considered very good investments."

"So she owned ground that somebody else rented."

"Yes," he replied. "They had what they called 'ninety-nine year leases.' And she inherited money from her aunts, who were ancient at the time. And some of their leases went back to the past century. 1870, you know."

"And this rented land was in Baltimore?" I asked.

Spies nodded. "Yes. The city of white steps. Almost all the houses over there—sort of row houses as a matter of fact— have white marble steps. And they're the pride and joy of the people who live there. They keep those steps in immaculate condition."

"I see. Now, these investments—your wife took care of them?"

Spies said, "Yes—well, after her folks died, she inherited money too. She took care of all their business."

"Would she collect the rent for those Baltimore properties? She must have."

"She'd collect it," he said. "She was very understanding of some people who couldn't make one payment—just a payment, once. They finally did pay. She never got the law on anybody.

"When Renice died, I had to do all of this work. It was quite a revelation to me to have to handle it. I got out of it as soon as I could because I didn't like to do that sort of thing."

I smiled. "You wanted to concentrate on your photography instead."

"Yes," Spies said. "I did."

"What were you working on then?"

"Well—I have to explain first—in 1967, I got involved in photographing the wild ponies of Chincoteague. I had seen them on television and found them quite intriguing. Every year the firemen of Chincoteague put on this pony swim. They own the ponies. In 1924 there was a fire which almost wiped out Chincoteague. And since then the firemen have used the money from the sale of these colts to buy fire equipment. Of course, they protect the horses as well.

"As it was, after photographing cats for 20 years, I was starting to get burned out. I was ready for a new challenge.

"I had for many years in the back of mind thought that I would like to go down to Chincoteague and try my hand at photographing the wild ponies. But when I actually decided to go, it was on the spur of the moment. Every hotel room I inquired about was taken for fifty miles away, in anticipation of the popular annual pony swim. I ended up staying in a hotel in Salisbury, Maryland, which is fifty miles from Chincoteague.

"The traffic down there was monumental, the roads jammed with tourists. It wasn't much better once you were out of the car. It was a small town, and you could hardly move.

"I had gotten up early and driven there so I'd find a good place to park. I took along some food and ate breakfast in my car. Afterwards, I went over to photograph the pony swim.

"It took the ponies fifteen minutes to swim from Assoteague to Chincoteague. Much to my dismay, I discovered that it was impossible to photograph the swim, because of the swarms of people. I was very disappointed.

"Then, I came upon this man, Ed Clark, who had a pony called Cloudy, the first grandson of the famous horse Misty, that was immortalized in the books written by Marguerite Henry. Ed was out in the back yard, getting Cloudy to perform. He loved to give this horse commands, and then Cloudy would do various tricks.

"I got out my camera equipment, thinking, 'Well, I'll photograph this procedure here, so I won't have a complete loss for my trip.' And I did. I became good friends with Ed Clark, a friendship which lasted until his death.

"I went down to Chincoteague for thirteen years to visit Ed and to photograph the wild horses. Each year, Ed would devise tricks for Cloudy to perform, that he wanted me to photograph."

"What sort of tricks would he do?" I asked.

"Oh, get down and bow his head, for example," Spies answered. "All sorts of things like that. And the children loved the pony and Ed too. Ed would do that at the drop of a hat for almost anyone who came along—it gave him that much pleasure."

"So," I said, "you took a lot of photos of the wild horses as well?"

Spies nodded. "I took many, many photographs of the wild horses."

"What sort of equipment did you use? What kind of lens?"

He paused. "I used a 30 mm lens on my Hassenblad camera. It was what's called a fish eye lens, and it provided me with an extreme depth of field."

I asked, "How soon did you realize you were going to have a book about the horses?"

"Well, I went down there for thirteen summers. Thirteen years. And somewhere toward the end of that time I got the idea that I would try to do a book, which I did. I seem to have books drop out all the time, and that's one that I first tried up in New York—to get a publisher—and it was cold. So that's where I dropped down to a second-rate publisher, maybe third-rate. But they were honest, at least."

"Now who was that?" I asked.

"Tidewater Publishing Co."

I commented, "All these trips—it seems to me that this photography required a great deal of energy."

"Yes, it can," Spies agreed. "And it takes patience. For example, at the beginning of the book, there's a beautiful picture of several ponies running directly toward me (see photo section). The ponies were rounded up and put in the coral. Now I had been told that this picture could only be obtained when they first came into the corral. That meant I had to be out there early for the beginning of the drive. There wouldn't be any picture, otherwise. Now I was told to be out there early because the drive would take place early. I ended up waiting until three o'clock to get that picture."

I asked, "Was it dangerous photographing these wild horses?"

"Oh yes," he said. "I took the greatest risks to my life as a photographer in taking pictures of those horses at Chincoteague. Stallions would be fighting in the corral, trying to protect their harems of mares, and I would get in the corral to take pictures. I wasn't supposed to do that, but I'd get in there anyway for the sake of getting a good picture. I would have to depend upon the stallion respecting and not hurting me—which you really couldn't count on one hundred percent. You can never tell what horses might do, particularly when they are excited and an unfamiliar human enters their territory.

"After one of my trips to Chincoteague," he said slowly, "I had an uncomfortably realistic dream in which a stallion is about to attack me. He is on his hind legs with his teeth showing. This is a dream I have had many times."

Obviously, these wild horses, terrible in their beauty and wildness, had struck a deep chord in Dr. Spies.

He continued, "On another occasion, I was photographing tigers in an enclosed area of King's Dominion, a theme park just north of Richmond, Virginia. Before I went in, I asked an attendant how I should react around the tigers. Lions basically ignore you, but tigers are different. They look you right in the eye—with malicious intent. They want to get you. The attendant explained that the tigers will follow a car around once you're inside the enclosure, and they'll actually jump up on the roof of the vehicle. He told me to use my own judgement. Of course, that's what they always say." He laughed scornfully.

"There were twelve or thirteen Siberian tigers in this enclosure. When the gate of that enclosure slammed behind me, I happened to be alone. For some reason, the attendant who was usually present was not on hand. These Siberian tigers were quite beautiful, a little bit lighter colored than the ordinary Bengal tiger—and I was eager to take photographs of them. But they looked menacing too. I said to myself, 'What in the devil am I doing in here with all these tigers?!' " And he chuckled.

"You were in a vehicle?"

Spies nodded. "Yes, my car. A number of the tigers did follow me as I drove around slowly, but I was not in any danger."

I said, "So you got some camera shots while you were in the car—did you roll down the window?"

"Yes, I almost always did," he responded. "We weren't supposed to do that either, but I did. I tried to keep an eye out, so none of them would sneak up on me.

"It was a reasonably safe adventure, and I got some good photos out of it. While I was there, I also photographed mature lions, as well as a baby tiger and two baby lions that were used for promotion in order to attract visitors to King's Dominion.

"While driving around in that enclosed tiger pen at King's Dominion did make me nervous, I was quite surprised at seeing the risks another photographer took at the Washington Zoo. There were two leopards in a screened in area of the zoo. The female was much more active than the male and would pace around. In addition to that screen fence, there was an additional protective fence about six feet away from the inside fence.

"I happened to see this foolhardy photographer jump over this outer fence in order to get a better shot of the leopards. That female leopard charged, literally flattening herself right up against that inside fence. The photographer was quite unnerved. I don't think he'll ever do anything like that again."

Dr. Spies chuckled, shaking his head. I could see the difference between him and that photographer. Spies was adventurous, but he wasn't a fool. He didn't take unnecessary chances.

"When I photographed animals at the Washington Zoo," Spies said, "I couldn't help noticing how most tourists made the same mistake when taking pictures. They had their flash on the same level as the lens of their camera, resulting in 'red eye.' The photographer would get a reflection of the color in the eyes of their subject, and the eyes would appear red in the picture. In order to get around that, I held the flash about thirteen inches or so above the lens of the camera. This would prevent 'red eye.' "

I asked, "Did you learn from other photographers? Did you belong to any photography clubs?"

Spies said, "For a while, I belonged to the USDA Photographic Round Table, which is similar to a camera club, except we thought we were kind of fancy. I used to lead that class. I learned a lot that way. In composition and techniques of photography and all."

"Would people bring in photographs they'd taken recently for others to critique?"

Spies nodded. "Yes, right. They didn't like me too much"—he smiled a little—"because I was too harsh."

"Too honest?" I suggested.

Spies shrugged his shoulders. Obviously, their approval—or disapproval—didn't mean that much to him. "Some people didn't like me. Some appreciated it."

"So you were highly critical?"

"Well, I was just honest, that's all," he said. "I didn't look at it as being highly critical. They should have appreciated that.

I didn't enjoy being harsh with them just to be unkind, but—"

"Did you get feedback from people about your photos?"

"Yes," he said.

I inquired, "And how did you feel it was different from a regular photography club?"

"Well, we went into more detail," he said. "For example, composition was one of the main things. Anyone can learn the techniques of photography, exposure, and so forth. That doesn't require any real creativity, but each photograph, the composition of each photograph, is what counts. Each one is different, so you have an infinite variety of problems."

"So you focused more on composition of photographs rather than specific technical aspects of photography."

"Yes," he said. "Technical aspects are sort of routine. But composition has—endless variety."

His voice became reverent when he said "endless variety."

I observed, "Well, that seems contradictory as to why you like chemistry."

"Well, in a way, it does, but it was sort of a relief to do photography." He added, grinning, "I'm not against relaxing."

So photography was a creative outlet for Spies, fulfilling him in a way that chemistry did not.

Spies continued, "I displayed my photographs in numerous exhibitions over the years. Probably my most prestigious exhibition was at the Smithsonian Institution in Washington D.C. And that was actually my first exhibition. I had considerable trouble getting it arranged. The fellow in charge of the exhibition was a little hesitant about having me show my work there because I didn't have a well known name."

"How did it come about?"

"I knew the director of the Smithsonian beforehand," Spies explained. "He had been involved in the selection of my pictures for *The Washington Star*. He knew my work.

"They held the exhibition in the Art and Industries Building of the Smithsonian in January and February of 1956, displaying fifty of my cat photographs. The exhibit was publicized in a number of newspapers, big and small." Spies looked down at his notes. "In the February '56 issue of *Ag Reporter*, the writer noted that, 'It is hard to decide whether Dr. Spies' hobby is photography or cats, but he combines them so beautifully that it doesn't make any difference.' "

Spies smiled, then continued his narrative. "I have felt quite proud of all of my exhibitions. But one exhibition in particular stands out. I showed my photographs and gave talks on cat photography in New York at the Cat Show of the Empire Cat Club on 34th Street. The first year I was scheduled to exhibit my work, there had been some disagreement among the members of the club as to whether I should be invited. And so I wasn't treated very well."

"Why not?" I asked. "Cat snobbery?"

Spies laughed, shrugging his shoulders. "I brought my slides and photographs, determined to do the best I could. Unfortunately, they put me in the regular exhibition room, which was huge. I had to speak through a microphone, with my voice booming through these loudspeakers. There was also no way to cut out the light entirely for showing my slides. To compensate, I put some sort of blanket over the screen. I did it all in good humor—sort of.

"I attended the show for seven years in a row. The last three or four years I took along my good friend and colleague Bill Stein, who assisted me."

"Where else did you exhibit your work?" I asked.

"I had three exhibitions at the Central Library of Arlington. For my second exhibit there in March, 1971, I selected 100 color prints." He consulted his notes. "I included purebred cats; my own pet cats, describing pictorially the nature of cats; and fantasy cats, showing eyes, faces, and silhouettes in unusual settings to illustrate the alleged occult nature of cats."

Later, when I was reading Spies's scrapbook, I came across a copy of the *Lensletter*, the newsletter for the USDA Photographic Round Table, in which the reporter noted that this was "probably one of the largest one-man photography exhibits of cats ever held in Washington, and certainly the largest color print show of cats in the area."

Spies continued, "Over the years I also gave numerous talks on animal photography to camera clubs and animal organizations. In October, 1981—just to give an example—I presented a slide show to the Cosmos Club in Washington, D.C. I showed slides of birds and animals in the backyard; ponies and wildlife on Chincoteague and Assateague Islands; animals at Kings Dominion; and birds and animals at the zoo in Washington. I wanted to show how a wide variety of animals to photograph could be found within 200 miles of Washington."

He leaned forward, looking excited. I knew Dr. Spies well enough by now to know he had an axe to grind, and it no doubt be ground to a fine, sharp edge.

"When I exhibited a number of my photographs at Tuft University, I wanted to use the photographs in which I show a cat 'reading' a Thornton Burgess book. Originally, when I first published those photographs, I had to get permission from Little Brown in Boston, which they readily gave. But when I wanted to get permission this time, I had to go to the inheritors of the Burgess estate. And, would you believe it, they wouldn't give permission for me to display these photos at Tuft. They were downright rude about it. So I gave up.

"For several years, I donated photographs to the Washington National Zoological Park for their annual silent auction, to help them raise money. One of my photographs sold for four hundred dollars."

This raised an interesting question. "Dr. Spies, did you try to sell your photographs, to market them?"

Spies shook his head. "I enjoyed getting my books and photographs published, but the commercial aspects of photography turned me off entirely. Oh, at one time, I did consider trying to sell my pictures at a department store, and I even went so far as to get a business license. But I couldn't bring myself to do it. Really, my only interest in regard to photography was to conceive the idea of a particular photograph and see if I could do it."

12

The Ups-and-Downs of Publishing

Dr. Spies said, "I sent my pictures out to a number of places, trying to get them published. Most people were honest, and I had corresponded with this one particular fellow near Boston without any problems—or so I thought. He seemed the essence of honesty. We tentatively discussed doing a calendar with my cat photographs in it; we had even determined a price. I sent a batch of photos to him, and I didn't hear any more from him.

"One day, some time later, a fellow says to me, 'Say, that's a nice calendar you got.'"

"I asked, 'Where'd you see that?'"

"He said he'd seen the calendar with my cat photographs in it in a display window of crafts in the YWCA. I purchased the calendar at the YWCA and then corresponded with this fellow again. He never answered my letters, although I kept hounding him. He beat me out."

I shook my head, saying, "That's terrible. I bet he made some money off that calendar."

Spies said, "I don't know whether he did or not. I kept hounding him. My brother Earl, who liked to take things into his own hands, said, 'Let's go down there and beat him up.' "

Spies laughed as he remembered.

"I said to Earl, 'Well, we'd be in more trouble then.' So he used the pictures, and I got absolutely nothing for them."

"That stinks," I said. "Anyway, the calendar looked great. So, how did you approach getting your books published?"

Spies sighed. "Each book I completed took me several years to get published. When I first went up to New York, I used to take my photographs in hand—loose, not even placed in an album—and show them to people. I was dismissed by the lowest people, assistants, who said, 'Look, get some of these pictures published before you come back to us.' So I worked on that hard, and I published a good number of them.

"I then put together a 135-page picture book, tentatively entitled *Jigger and Her Kittens*, which I submitted to a number of publishers.

"I was rejected several times. But, finally, I had a good piece of news. I heard from an editor for Studio Publications, an offshoot of a New York publishing company, Thomas Y. Crowell. This editor approved my photographs for a book, but he told me I had write a text to accompany them."

I commented, "Your cat books—or your animal books, in general—included a lot of information, for example, how to take photos of cats, how to care for cats. I mean, with the cat books, there's quite a bit of information on cats, generally speaking."

"Oh yes," Spies responded.

"Did you research all this?"

Spies nodded. "My first book, when I started writing my cat book, I used to just go in this room"—he pointed to a small den behind him—"go to my desk, write and turn off all the television and radio and so forth. That was the only way to get it done.

"I visited the home of the publisher of *Cats Magazine*, Raymond Smith, to have him review the manuscript of this first book. Raymond lived in Washington, Pennsylvania. He and his wife had long been involved with cats. His wife was a judge of cat shows. So it was somewhat surprising to me when I discovered that Raymond had a good-sized dog waiting to greet me, that he had loose. And you know, that dog came right up to me and bit me hard on the buttocks."

He laughed.

"That wasn't a very friendly dog," I commented.

"No, it wasn't," he said. "When I told Raymond about it, he just laughed. But this dog—I didn't know what to do. Usually, with a dog, if you just stand there and do not make any sudden moves, it won't bother you. But he did, and I didn't know whether to start fighting back or not because you wouldn't want to do that if you're a guest in somebody's home.

"As soon as I got a chance, I went into the bathroom and took down my trousers to see what damage the dog had done. Sure enough, there was a mark." He laughed.

I said, "It's ironic—this guy was the publisher for *Cat Magazine*? And he had a dog greeting you?"

Spies laughed even harder. "That is rather ironic. At any rate, Raymond became a great friend of mine.

"Eventually, I did succeed in getting that first book published. It didn't end up being called *Jigger and Her Kittens*, however. With the accompanying text that included extensive explanations of how I took the pictures, it made more sense to title the book, *Cats and How I Photograph Them.*

"Now, this fellow that was a scam artist on the calendar, he almost kept me from getting the book published. This New York editor—I forget the name of the company just now—had accepted my manuscript for publication, and I was very excited.

"I was still in his office at the time, when it occurred to me that I had all these pictures submitted to the man who was going to publish the calendar. I'd forgotten about that, believe it or not.

"I immediately told the editor, and he said, 'That's bad. I guess we can't do it.' Then he went into his office and stayed there for a little while and talked to somebody on the phone about it. He came out of his office and said, 'We'll try to beat him. We'll try to publish them before he does.' That was the story of how I almost lost the publication of my first book—to a swindler."

I commented, "You know, they probably could have nailed him. If the calendar came out after the book."

"Well, that's right, they could," he said. "Copyright infringement."

After I left Dr. Spies that day, I opened the book of newspaper clippings and read what a number of reviewers had to say about Dr. Spies' first cat book. Comments were mostly positive.[12]

Arguably, the book received the highest praise in the July '58 issue of *Harper's Magazine*, in which the reviewer said this is "a book that both photographers and cat-lovers will take to their hearts," actually called the book "entrancing," and added that "the photographs of cats and kittens are as surprising and beautiful as any I've seen." This same reviewer expressed a preference for the "natural" pictures as opposed to the "posed" ones, which suggests that some of the photographs were more successful than others, since all of them were "posed" in some sense.

When I met with Dr. Spies again, he explained, "As I told you, I had decided not to look at other cat books or similar books until I had my very first book published. I didn't want to be influenced at that point. But after the publication of *Cats and How I Photograph Them*, I started taking courses. From then on, I found out what I was doing wrong. I made a study of composition—the arrangement of the components of a picture. And so I kept improving on the composition of my photographs for many years."

I asked, "Is there anyone's work that you especially admire in photography? A photographer who inspired you or whom you imitated?"

"No," he said, grinning. "I suppose I was somewhat of an egotist. I didn't feel I needed to follow somebody."

"At that point," he continued, "I decided to get more ambitious and try to publish a book of purebred cats. That really required a lot of work.

"First, I designed an apparatus I called my Portable Cat Photography Studio, so I could photograph cats with greater ease at cat shows. I built my 'studio,' using plywood and some discarded rods and clamps from the chemistry laboratory. I designed it so it could be disassembled, transported by automobile, and later reassembled quickly.

"The colored backgrounds and bases were changeable; I could use blue or green or brown as the background or base for the photograph—whatever I needed as a background color to be complimentary to the color of the cat. I arranged four electronic flashlights in key locations, two lighting the background, one located above, and one a direct light.

"I also wanted to standardize the setting of the exposure to be the same for both color and black-and-white. That required me to get a new camera. I purchased a Hassenblad 1000F, which has a removable film back."

"What's the advantage of that?" I asked.

"You can take the film off in the middle of a roll and replace it with another roll of either black-and-white or color film," Spies answered. "This gave me the freedom to photograph cats with ease in both color and black-and-white in one sitting. I could also use either transparencies or print film.

"In this way, I standardized as much as I could on the Portable Cat Photography Studio so I wouldn't have to do anything but photograph cats.

"I tried out my Portable Studio for a whole year at home, so I couldn't fail when I attended a cat show. Finally, I felt ready. I went to a cat show out in Hyattsville, Maryland. I engaged the services of a young woman who knew something about purebred cats, Shirley Pfeiffer. And I had my chemical assistant to help me also.

"I photographed over twenty strange cats that weekend. These were cats that I had never seen before."

"Different breeds of cats?"

"Yes. But, being show cats, they were used to handling. I took twenty-two pictures in both color and black-and-white.

"I struck a deal with the owners of these cats. They had to sign a release form I carried with me, to allow me to use the photographs for books and magazines."

I asked, "Did they get anything in return?"

"Oh, in the release it said I would give them a dollar—which I didn't, but that's just a legal formality. Instead, I gave each cat owner a 11" by 14" picture, mounted—a beautiful black and white picture."

"Wow," I exclaimed, "that's a lot better than a dollar!"

Spies nodded. "Yes, they appreciated that very much. At that time there was a lot of mistrust of photographers because they had used pictures in advertising when they didn't have permission to do so, and all sorts of other scams. So the first thing I did, as soon as I took those photographs, was to make the 11" by 14" pictures and give them to each individual that I had a contract to do it with. It soon helped to dispel that mistrust. I was much sought after from then on.

"So, my work along this line required me to make various trips. For example, I went up to Erie, Pennsylvania, which is right at the end of Lake Erie. I traveled to people's homes and took pictures of their cats. I took pictures of famous cats too."

"Like Caroline Kennedy's cat," I said.

"She was later," he responded. "I didn't use that apparatus for that, but yes, I did take pictures of that cat."

"Can you tell me about that? How did it come about?"

Spies smiled. "Well, that's rather interesting. There was a young woman who used to write stories about cats, and it was her idea to do a feature on Tom Kitten, Caroline Kennedy's cat. During the Kennedy White House days, Tom Kitten was getting quite a bit of publicity—almost as much as Socks [President Clinton's cat] nowadays. So this young woman contacted me to see if I would photograph Tom Kitten, and then she would write the story. I agreed to do that.

"We were hoping to get in the White House, but in the meantime, the Kennedys had sent Tom Kitten to live with Jackie Kennedy's personal secretary, Mary Gallagher, who lived in Alexandria, Virginia. So we went to Ms. Gallagher's house and I photographed Tom Kitten. Got beautiful pictures. One ended up on the cover of *Cats Magazine* in—in June, 1961. I also sent a large, mounted picture to Mrs. Kennedy through this personal secretary of hers. And I got a nice letter in reply, you know, from the President's wife."

"That's thrilling!" I myself would have loved to have received a letter from Jackie Kennedy.

"Well, it was thrilling—I suppose," Spies said. "But then Mrs. Kennedy got kind of mad when she found out about the cover on *Cats Magazine*. She felt we were exploiting her. I had also made the statement that Tom Kitten looked like—there's a breed of cat called Russian Blue—and I made the statement that this looked like a Russian Blue. Jean Strohl quoted me in her article, in which I dared to joke about his resemblance to a Russian Blue, saying it 'might have been to blame for his leaving the White House!' That didn't sit very well with the Kennedy's, because of the touchy situation with Communist Russia at that time."

I shook my head. "That's ridiculous."

Spies finished, "Anyway, that ended our friendship—brief though it was. We didn't get to meet Caroline or John-John, as he was called. I don't know if it would have made any difference."

He added, "We kept track of Tom Kitten and learned that he eventually died of cirrhosis of the liver. I've never heard of a cat getting that. Maybe he became an alcoholic when he was…"

"Living with the Kennedys?" I suggested.

Spies laughed. "Yeah. We probably shouldn't be saying this."

I looked down at my notes. "So, back to your work on the purebred cats—"

Spies said, "I continued work on my second book during this time, concentrating on getting up-to-date photographs of the various breeds of cat. At this time there were only eleven breeds. Now there are many more than that—twenty-five or thirty. And in each breed, there were many colors. For example, the Persian Cat—I think there were about twenty-five different colors.

"When I took photographs for my book, I didn't get examples of each color; that would have been too much. I just got one color example of the particular breed and maybe a black one.

"Years later, long after the first edition of *The Compleat Cat* was published, people said that my book provided a historical record of how cats used to be, when there were only eleven breeds. Later, of course, I had a revised edition of the same book printed, and I included many more breeds, of different colors. I think there are probably twenty-five or thirty breeds now."

I asked, "Did you get the book published right away?"

Spies shook his head. "I had rejection after rejection, for years, with *The Compleat Cat*. Finally, Prentice-Hall got interested.

"When I was first going to meet with Prentice-Hall, I told them I was going to bring a lot of pictures. They said, 'Don't do that.' They probably thought they were going to have to reject them. Fortunately, that isn't what happened. They liked the pictures very much.

"When they actually decided to publish the book, the editor, Edgar Best, came to Washington D.C. and took my wife, Renice, and me to dinner. And they kept us informed of the progress with getting the book printed. Other companies don't do that. They're the only publisher I've dealt with since that time that I considered treated me as a human being, without contempt."

"That's unfortunate," I commented.

"It is," Spies said. "The first edition was entitled *The Compleat Cat: The Private Life of the Cat—From Kittenhood to Courtship*." He checked his notes. "The book was published in November of 1966, just in time for Christmas. This was ideal timing, because newspapers across the United States reviewed it, often recommending it as a good Christmas gift."

In looking through Dr. Spies' scrapbook of newspaper clippings, I discovered he received much more publicity on this second book, most of it reviews containing glowing praise.

Dr. Spies' friend Raymond Smith, the publisher of *Cat Magazine*, called it "one of the great all-time books of the cat world." He may have have a little prejudiced, but he was far from being alone in his opinion.

The World in Books said, "Dr. Spies' book, *The Compleat Cat*, with its many polished facets, sparkles like a diamond. The photographs are magnificent, the information encyclopedic and fully indexed, and the literary style superb," adding "it would enhance anyone's library."

Fort Wayne, Indiana's *News Sentinel* said, "The handsomest animal book of the year is Joseph R. Spies' *The Compleat Cat*," adding that "the pictures are attractive enough to cut out and frame and the prose is perceptive and completely informative."

There may have been an implied criticism in the December 1, 1966 review by *The Christian Science Monitor*: "Prize-winning cat photographs, photographs of prize-winning cats, and photographs that could win a prize for pure schmaltz, together with a text covering every aspect of cat care should make this qualify as the cat handbook of the year." This reviewer was not necessarily a lover of cats.

In their article on cats, Compton's *Encyclopedia Year Book* (1966) mentions the book, saying, "The cat-book event of the year was the publication of *The Compleat Cat*, by Joseph R. Spies, which contains color plates of all show cat breeds. It was the first such book to appear since 1903."

In addition to all of this print publicity, Dr. Spies was interviewed by Barbara Walters on "The Today Show" on November 22, 1966, catapulting his cat-ographer fame.

Spies said, "Prentice-Hall had helped to arrange the interview initially. At first, it looked as if the interview would be cancelled because of news time devoted to President Johnson's illness and because of a strike going on in New York at the time. But the interview remained on the schedule.

"I chose one of our household cats to take to New York, making sure to select one that had the right disposition and temperament for such a trip." He held up a picture of the cat he took on the trip.

I said, "She's a gorgeous cat." And she was, long-haired, graceful, and calm in her demeaner.

Spies said, "This is a Maine Coon cat. She's not a purebred, but she's the type of a Maine Coon cat. They're famous for their pleasant dispositions and their loving relationships with people."

"She looks a little irritated in this picture."

Spies laughed. "No, no."

I asked, "Are there some of your cats that you wouldn't have selected for that trip to New York?"

"Oh yes, there's some—she was ideal," he said. "I selected her because I thought she had the best personality."

"Did you prepare her in any way for the trip?"

"Oh, I took Simba for drives, and I also walked her in the park on a leash. But that was basically it.

"I also selected a number of color and black-and-white photographs for use on the show. I had decided not to send them ahead of time, not trusting the mail to be reliable. I drove to New York, taking these cat pictures."

I asked, "How did Simba do on the trip?"

"Oh, wonderful," he said enthusiastically. "She did great. She went to New York with me in a cat carrying cage, and we were on the tenth floor of a hotel. Forget what the name of it was now. I went to bed early, because we had to be at the studio at five o'clock in the morning. During the night, I woke up and saw her sitting at the window, looking out at New York.

"Simba never got scared or anything; she trusted me completely. When I took her over to the studio, she stayed quite calm. She even had a little dressing room there." He laughed. "A room by herself."

"She did?" I was astounded. "Her own dressing room?"

"Well—" Spies laughed—"she didn't dress, but she did have a room to herself.

"Neither Barbara Walters nor her partner Huge Downs wanted to conduct this interview. Neither of them was enthusiastic about cats.

"When I sat down before the camera with Simba on my lap— behaving just beautifully—Barbara started out by saying, 'I would like to have you know I don't like cats.' That was her first statement." He chuckled.

"I should have said, 'I'm sorry. It's your loss.' But we did get along very well and had a nice interview. When we were done, she even reached over rather gingerly and petted Simba on the head.

"All of this publicity paid off. The first edition of *The Compleat Cat* sold out within two months of publication, and Prentice-Hall followed it up with a second printing."

This was no doubt the height of Dr. Spies' cat-photographer fame.

He continued, "During this time, I gave numerous talks on what it takes to get a book published. With the publication of my second book, I had learned much. That's when the real work begins—after you've written the manuscript and taken the pictures. Trying to get a book published can only be described as real, honest-to-God drudgery. You have to have the hide of a rhinoceros." He sighed. "You will get rejected—I've had rejection and rejection.

"Years later, Prentice-Hall would ask me to revise *The Compleat Cat*, which I did, including a number of color photographs by some other cat photographers as well as some recent ones of my own that had not been published in the first edition. Raymond Smith wrote the foreword to this revised edition, which seemed most appropriate, since he had always been an avid supporter of my work and over the years published many of my photographs in *Cats Magazine*. But then Prentice-Hall insisted on having a professional writer rewrite my manuscript, and they wanted to list this writer as a second author on the cover.

"I was vehemently opposed to having someone tinker with my text and get credit for it on the cover. They wanted to make him a second author. I was so upset, in fact, that I called them and said that the deal was off—I didn't want to publish the book. But, eventually, we reached a compromise, in which this writer only received recognition in the acknowledgements.

"I must admit," Spies added grudgingly, "[the writer] did polish the writing. He lightened things up a bit from the original text, making it more readable to most people, I guess."

"When was the second edition published?"

He said, "I think it was 1984 ... the same year that my wife died."

Dr. Spies received a number of good reviews for this second edition, although not as many this time around.

Cat World commented on the improvements in this second edition, saying that it was "a little more streamlined, the color plates reflecting advances in film and color reproduction, the breeds section reflecting the added breeds, the greater number of shows, more of everything in the cat fancy." This reviewer concluded, "If it is possible to present the compleat cat in 223 pages with pen and camera, this welcome update of an older, standard cat fancy reference book does so."

During my interviews with Dr. Spies, I said, "I think I've got in my notes somewhere that *The Compleat Cat* was translated into Italian?"

"Oh yes," he said.

"*Il Mio Amico Gatto—My Friend the Cat*. How did that happen?"

"Well, Prentice-Hall did that for me. I didn't even know at first that they did it. They made arrangements with an overseas publisher for my book to be published in Italian I think I received over eight hundred dollars for the translation, and it was a great thrill for me. I wanted to get some extra copies, so I corresponded with the Italian publisher. And to get about 50 copies cost roughly about 60,000 lira."

"How much is 60,000 lira?" I asked.

Spies grinned. "Well, it's not much. It just sounds big, you know."

"Yeah, it does. But why Italian? That's what I was wondering. Why not Spanish or French or something else?"

"I don't know," Spies said. "I guess Italians like cats better than any other group—although the French are supposed to be great cat lovers also.

"I worked with the Italians on another occasion, when an article illustrated with eleven of my pictures of ponies at Chincoteague and Assateague was published in the September 1984 issue of *Atlante*, an Italian version of *National Geographic*. The reproduction of those pictures exceeded anything that I had seen before, and I was quite pleased.

"About the same time as the printing of the second edition of *The Compleat Cat*, Simon and Schuster took over Prentice-Hall in a great western finance deal. And they acted as though—I'm sure they beat me out. I never got the royalties I should have had from that second edition. Prentice-Hall had also accepted my last book, *Big Cats and Other Animals: Their Dignity, Beauty, and Survival*, but Simon and Schuster turned it down.

I said, "You must have felt frustrated."

"I was," he said.

"Now, about your second book ...."

"Are you going to ask if getting the first book published helped with the second?" Spies responded. "It didn't. Not with the second, or the third or the fourth, for that matter. Each was a struggle onto itself. I've never seen anyone as tough as an editor can be.

"I used to use *The Literary Marketplace* as the Bible for getting the telephone number of the appropriate editor. I would call them, tell them my story, and ask them if they wanted to see the manuscript. If they said yes, I sent them a letter of transmittal, plus a number of pictures. And they would consider them.

"Once, after sending a publisher a letter and some pictures, I got them rejected almost by return mail. It is really amazing that they could do it that fast. Of course, I would always include postage. I would send it by express mail and include postage for express mail return. I always did things first class by sending it by the top mail that I could use."

I asked, "How many rejections did you get before you got your first book published?"

"I really don't know," he said. "I can say it was a lot. After a rejection, I would feel hurt for a few days. Then I would get my confidence back and send them in again. And I would keep that up."

"Did you ever get comments?"

"Oh yes," he said. "With some I would get comments that I could use for improvement. With my next-to-last book, *Wild Ponies of Chincoteague*, I did try the New York scene for publishing and found that I would only get so far. When several editors rejected it, I assumed all of them would."

"So I moved down a notch, from the New York scene to a smaller publisher from the eastern shore where that famous horse Misty lived, Tidewater Publishers in Cambridge, Maryland. I think I mentioned them earlier. That is, actually, how I got *Wild Ponies of Chincoteague* published in 1977."

He consulted his notes again. "The book contained approximately 120 pages of text and ninety-nine black and white photographs. This small publisher had to refuse the color photographs because of the expense of printing in color. It was fortunate that I had taken so many photographs in black and white."

This time Dr. Spies received only a few reviews.

In a November 17, 1977 issue of Arlington's newspaper, *The Globe*, the writer praised the horse photographs, saying, "Spies was afforded opportunities to capture on film the Chincoteague ponies as no one, before or since, has been able to photograph them." Native Sun Books, in their winter 1985 issue, recommended the book, saying, "The text describing the events and their history is for a proficient reader, but anyone who loves horses will enjoy the pictures."

I asked, "Out of the books that you've done, how does this book fit into the scheme of things?"

"Well, they're animals," he said, laughing. "Just like lions, tigers, etc. I love all animals. Now, with the book *Big Cats and Other Animals*, I went down yet another notch in the publishing field. I was getting anxious because of my age. I couldn't play the waiting game any longer because I didn't know what was going to go first—me or the book. So I offered to pay him—what do they call it?"

"Subsidized?" I suggested.

Spies nodded. "Yeah. Partial. I asked him if he would do that, and he said he would. And so I paid thousands of dollars—before it was all said and done—to an editor in Florida who turned out to be less than honest. He did me out of quite a bit of money. I never got one cent of royalties out of it. But I don't mind because I did get a very good book out of it, thanks to a woman who worked in that organization.

"This editor was a man who was more concerned about his shoestring than anything else. He looked for a place to reproduce the color for the book, and he found such a place in Columbia, South America. Do you know my transparencies were held up because the authorities discovered there was a cocaine shipment on the plane?"

"You're kidding," I said. As if Dr. Spies hadn't already been through enough with these jerks....

"No, it's the truth," Spies said. "The authorities wouldn't release my photos for a long time. The publisher really had to work to get them. That was just one problem, however.

"We planned on having the book out by a certain Christmas. At that time I was having carotid artery operations, but I was still doing everything I could to get them to get the book done. They kept stringing me along, stalling until the last part of November. And they still hadn't printed the book.

"Finally, the publisher told me about Thanksgiving time that the book would be delayed, that it probably wouldn't be published until May. That's when I could stand it no longer.

"I jumped in my car and drove from Washington D.C. to Yellowstone Park." He laughed at himself. "At that time, I just had to, because I needed something to tear me away from my thinking, because I couldn't stand these delays any more."

"That would be really frustrating," I agreed.

"What's more," Spies said, "the printer in Iowa told me he was sick and tired of me inquiring about the book all the time. I never talked to him after that. Instead, I talked to the publisher down in Florida who would then talk to the printer.

"In addition to all those problems, this publisher had a

publicity man to whom I had also paid money, who did nothing to publicize my book once it was printed. The publisher promised me that he would make up for this fellow who beat me out of my 'publicity' money. But before he did that, he went bankrupt. And I never received a cent. I'm not going to tell you the amount because it was quite a bit that I paid him. That's when I say that what happened to me shouldn't happen to a dog."

I simply shook my head. Spies' experiences, I suspect, are typical of people trying to get published.

Spies continued, "You would think, with all the problems I had, that I would have gotten a horrible book. But the woman who actually put the book together did a wonderful job. In essence, I had given her the manuscript and the photographs, and she arranged the manuscript in a way that was complimentary to the photographs.

"I called the woman and complimented her on the work she had done. I never spoke with that printer again. I certainly didn't compliment him on the book." He picked up a copy of the book and handed it to me. "The book contains fifty full-color photographs and 150 black-and-white photographs."

Looking at the book carefully, I was impressed by the photographs of these zoo animals. But I had to wince at the price—$29.95 cloth.

"This particular book, unfortunately, was not well received," Spies said. "I did get a few good reviews, but not from any significant sources. I really feel the reviewers who gave it a bad rating did not judge the book on its own merit. They looked down on it because I used a subsidy publisher."

In going through Dr. Spies' scrapbook later, I discovered a noteworthy review. Sheila Kinkade, in the April 2, 1990 issue of *The Washington Times*, praised the book, saying, "Mr. Spies waxes pleasantly on the tremendous potential of zoos to enhance our appreciation of animals and save the endangered ones" and added that, "many of the animals photographed in this book appear to be in their natural environs, so resplendent are the backdrops."

13

Animal Rights Activist and World Traveler

Spies began, "Before man disappears from this world because he has gotten rid of himself, I think that he will have killed all the animals also. Some of my friends at Tufts University feel more optimistic. They think that things may turn around completely, and that we have to depend on the education of children for this.

"However, all children are not educated. And there are enough uneducable children in the world, there's always going to be—as a matter of fact, one night on television I saw a story about man who poached in Yellowstone Park, killing elk. He went in there all the time and poached, and what's more, made video tapes of the killing and commercialized it. They finally caught him, but not before he had killed many elk—beautiful elk. That person deserves the death penalty. I know that may sound radical, but that's the way I feel about it."

I said,"It's interesting—I was thinking about what you just said in relation to how many Native Americans feel. They view it in perhaps a different way—"

"Oh yes, they do," he responded.

"As a part of their sacred tradition."

Spies nodded. "Yes, they almost apologize for killing them for food, you know."

"I've always thought we could learn a few things from them."

"Oh, of course, we could," Spies said. "But we won't. Believe me." And he laughed rather cynically for him. This was obviously a subject about which he felt very strongly.

"We certainly haven't learned anything up to this point," I said. "Dr. Spies, I'd like to hear about those radio talk shows you were on."

Spies said, " I used to be interviewed on radio talk shows, discussing this very issue. There's a publication, where you put such-and-such-a-statement in this publication and that circulates to all the radio stations. And they see the topic and the person who says things about the topic. That's the way they picked them out. And then they would call that person to arrange an interview on their particular radio station."

I said, "I looked at a flyer in your scrapbook, with the headline, 'Interview the Man'..."

"Oh yes, that's what I'm talking about," Spies said. "It was a one-page article, 'Interview the Man Who Believes Sports Hunters Are the World's Lowest Creatures'—that was me, of course. The article went on to explain briefly my views about hunting and animals and provided a phone number where I could be reached for radio interviews.

"I was interviewed on radio stations all over the country thirteen different times, from my home. The radio station would make arrangements ahead of time and then call me up to interview me.

"The second time I talked on the radio was in Grand Junction, Colorado. The two other speakers were the president of the Bow Hunters Club and an official of Colorado, and they were dead set against me. And I had a very hard time." He chuckled. "I hung in there and did the best I could, as I always do. My opponents regarded animals mainly as objects for bow hunting, trophy hunting, and other sports hunting. I cannot believe—I still can't believe—that they were representative of the people of Colorado.

"Another time, a radio station from Tucson, Arizona, KNST, was supposed to call and interview me. We had a misunderstanding about the time. I thought it was supposed to be the next day when they would be calling to interview me. Imagine my surprise when I get a call at three o'clock in the morning.

"Can you picture my being asleep, having the phone ring, getting up, and trying to conduct...anyway, I said, 'I can't do this. I thought it was the next morning.'

"He said, 'Well, you're going to leave us in a one hell of a spot if you don't do it.'

" 'The show must go on,' I answered finally. "I'll do the best I can.'

"And I did. I took it on.

"Did it go okay?" I asked.

Spies shrugged his shoulders. "Sort of, although I think I got cut off at the end because I got carried away and decided to call somebody contemptible." He grinned.

"That would be controversial?" It didn't seem to me to be such a terrible thing to say. I seriously doubted that name-calling was taboo on the air.

"Yes, I suspect it be controversial," he said. "Now, I want to say this: my experience at Grand Junction, Colorado—that was the worst interview, partly because it was only the second one. But later on, I think, about seventy-five or eighty percent of the people took my view instead of the opposite view. They were all for animals. So that was heartening to have that happen.

"Being interviewed on the radio, having these extraneous conversations, was not really my cup of tea. I don't like confrontation under those circumstances. But it was an opportunity to express my views about the protection of animals to the public."

I decided it was time to bring up a touchy point in his stance on the protection of animals. "Many animal rights activists are opposed to using animals in scientific research. Dr. Spies, why do you, unlike these other animal rights activists, support it?"

He said slowly, "It is something I had to come to grips with personally, because I used hundreds of—thousands of guinea pigs and rabbits and also—well, I didn't use rabbits, but other people who needed them in the lab did.

"But I looked down upon them. I mean, I would not have done those experiments on cats or dogs, not monkeys, or higher animals. I distinguished between guinea pigs and rats and—rabbits are sort of in between. And that was the way I was able to reconcile that. Now, the People for the Ethical Treatment of Animals, which is a very active, pro-animal rights group, they think all animals are equal."

I said, "Were the guinea pigs and rabbits in pain? I mean—did they suffer during the experiments?"

"No, no," he said. "We killed them swiftly, usually with a blow to the head or neck, before we began our work on them. My colleague Bill Stein did not mind killing them, but when he was not there, the responsibility fell on my shoulders. My assistant, Mary Ann Stevan, absolutely refused to do it. I can't say that I blame her."

"You may consider this a private matter, but I'll bring it up anyway. Is there a Christian perspective in all this? You said you were a Baptist growing up. Are you still Baptist or Christian?"

"No, I guess I'm agnostic," he replied. "That's my religion—if that's a religion. I hope for the best for a future life, but I doubt that there will be. That's the way I feel about it. As a matter of fact, a religious person who believes in an afterlife has it over someone like myself, because people like me are troubled all the time. Believers have this burden lifted from them. They know everything's going to be just like they say. And they let it go at that."

"It's true," I said. Dr. Spies and I were more alike than I'd realized. I'd had these same doubts and come to these same conclusions—perhaps more reluctantly than he had.

Spies said, "Now, if I'd accept that, I'd be delighted because— I don't say that I worry about it actively, but I do think about it. It does disturb me some."

"Yes, I've got to admit—I've known these people with this 'pure faith.'"

He nodded. "Yes, and they've got you in religion, because it's only by faith that you can enter the kingdom of Heaven."

"Which isn't something logical."

"No—it isn't." He laughed and turned back to our original topic. Obviously, he didn't consider it fruitful to discuss religion since it was nothing you could prove nor disprove. "You know, getting back to animal rights I watch Rush Limbaugh sometimes. You ever hear of him?"

I made a face. "I'm afraid I got so irritated listening to him one night—"

Spies laughed. "Well, you have to take him with a grain of salt. But I think, with his perspective, with his thoughts about animals, that they're simply horrible. For example, they had this thing on TV which they repeatedly showed on his program, of cutting up and killing a lobster and putting it in a frying pan. It was moving around while it was dying. And he loves that. Now I don't object to that for a person who is using it as food, but I don't see why anyone should just take pleasure in that sort of thing. See what I mean?"

"Yeah, I do. He was cooking it just to get a rise out of animal activists."

Spies said, "And I despise him for that. But—he has some pretty good points." He chuckled. "Okay, enough of that."

He had stated his views on Rush Limbaugh quite plainly, just as he had stated his views on religion. And he was done. Dr. Spies would not have made a very good philosopher, in my opinion.

Changing the subject I said, "I meant to ask you earlier— your wife accompanied you on a few of your trips, right?"

Spies shook his head. "Not very many. There was that one where we went to New York and stayed at the Waldorf-Astoria."

"Did she enjoy herself?"

"Oh yes," he said, nodding. "She would have liked to have traveled, but—"

"It was hard to do—for both of you?"

"Well—we had this family of cats." Spies laughed.

"Oh yeah, that's right," I said. "You had as many as thirteen at one time, right?"

"Yes, we did."

"That's incredible," I commented. "That's like having a family of thirteen children."

He responded, "It is, just about. The only time I wept during all those years was when I had to bury—I buried most of them in the back yard—the cats. And I always cried. It was terrible, just like a child.

"Whenever one would pass away.'

"Yes, yes," he said. I could swear he was holding back tears.

I responded, "People can get very attached to their animals and regard them as family members."

"Yes. No doubt about it."

I asked, "Now, did you tease your cats at all?"

"No, not in the sense of making them mad," he said.

"A lot of people love to do that."

"Oh, I know," he said. "Pull their tail and stuff. I didn't do that. As a matter of fact, we always treated our cats like children, with respect. We respected their personalities. We had to make the adjustments—not them."

"It's funny—wouldn't you say that people in the rural areas, on farms, look at cats differently than people in cities? They don't see them as pets?"

Spies nodded in agreement. "As working cats to keep down rats. Oh yeah, there are people that regard them that way. But they usually treat them pretty well.

"There are a number of people who enjoy torturing cats and so forth. In Washington, for example, I rescued this cat. This woman was tempted to let them out right in the middle of an intersection, of a busy street. And she was just about ready to let them out. Instead, she did bring them across the street and let them out."

"What made her change her mind, I wonder?"

"Oh, a spark of humanity, I suppose," he said. "I managed to catch one of them and bring it home. The others I never caught or saw again.

"One interesting thing—to shed some light on my wife—she one time adopted a stray female, who happened to be pregnant. She kept it in our home until the cat had her litter of babies. Renice let the kittens stay with their mother until they were old enough to leave her, and then she found homes for every one of the kittens, as well as their mother. At that time, we already had many cats of our own and couldn't really keep this bunch permanently."

I asked, "Can you tell me about this cat shelter you've got in back?"

"Oh yes." He looked toward the kitchen window. "When we first started getting a 'herd' of our own cats, we created a shelter for them that was quite comfortable. It consisted of 420 square feet, securely walled and roofed with a chain-link fence, in an L-shaped area that wrapped around two sides of my garage. We provided two aluminum shelters heated by electric coils, so the cats could stay warm even in the most severe of winter weather.

"We never had a young cat put to sleep. I almost did once, but the veterinary saved me. The cat had a hernia, an abdominal hernia that broke loose, and it was in terrible pain. And I took it over to the vet to have it put to sleep. And do you know he operated on that cat during the night and..."

"In the middle of the night?"

"Yes, and saved me from becoming a murderer." He laughed at his dramatic statement, but I could tell he felt very deeply about this.

"You must have been quite relieved."

"I was," he answered.

"I guess you don't think about cats having those kinds of ailments. It's interesting that you were able to combine having the cats in your house with photography. Now—when did you start taking your trips and photographing?"

"I didn't take any trips until after my wife passed away," he replied. "My first trip was made in June of 1986, and we went to Griese Fiord. And that's the farthest northern settlement in the western hemisphere."

"Why did you choose to go there?"

"Well"— he shrugged his shoulders—"that's where I wanted to go—go north. To the Northwest Territories."

I asked, "What attracted you to it? Rather than, say, going south at that time or somewhere else?

Again, he shrugged his shoulders. I think it rather delighted him that he did not have a good reason for going there. "Because I wanted to go to the Arctic."

I pressed, "Any specific reason?"

"No, just a hankering."

"For adventure?" I was desperate.

His face brightened. "Oh yes. On all of these trips I was primarily interested in animal photography. I signed on with a company that did tours there, called Special Odyssey. My friend Bill Stein accompanied me on a few of the trips. I took him to Alaska, Australia, and Patagonia."

I asked, "What sort of camera equipment did you bring with you?"

"Let's see..." he paused, "at home, I used a Hassenblad camera. You get better pictures. But, because it was too heavy to take on a trip like this. I switched to the Minolta."

"Because it was lighter-weight?"

He nodded. "Yes. And I took along several lenses. I did not use a tripod, as I was able to hold the camera in such a position that I wouldn't get any camera movement."

"Were you able to use the same kind of film as always, in this extreme cold?"

"I took slides, using Ectochrome 400 film," he answered. "A few critics said I would have done better with the slower-speed Kodachrome for scenery, but I felt this film was satisfactory."

"How did you get started on your trip?" I asked.

"To get to Griese Fiord, we first traveled to Montreal. Then we took a plane—a bush pilot's small plane, relatively." He frowned. "They call them something to do with otters—the Twin Otter—that's it."

I said, "So you took this type of plane from Montreal, and you went to this place, Griese Fiord?"

"Eventually, we ended up at Griese Fiord," Spies said, "although we stopped at a number of places along the way. I don't remember all of it. I do remember our departure from Griese Fiord was delayed because of 70 m.p.h. winds at the place where we were supposed to land. So we stayed at Griese Fiord all day.

"About seven o'clock in the evening, the tour guides decided the winds had subsided so we could make the trip. However, up there, the sun stays up until two or three o'clock in the morning. You had kids playing outside until midnight—in 'day' light. So we decided—not we, the people running the thing—decided to take off at that time, and the sun looked absolutely beautiful. Because the sun is so near the horizon at this time, you get wonderful photographs with these deep shadows.

"We flew over this place called Devon Island, which is mountainous. It got very rough going over the mountains, so rough that we would almost hit the ceiling of the plane at times. And I'm subject to air sickness, and I vomited and all that. But I was so excited at the beauty of the scenery that I somehow overcame it and managed to take pictures. The mountains were a beautiful sight. And lighted so beautifully. I didn't think I could recover that well from air sickness."

How many people in their eighties could travel to the Arctic for the first time in their lives? And be able to appreciate the beautiful scenery in spite of feeling sick? Once again, I had to admire Dr. Spies for what he had been able to accomplish.

Spies continued his narrative. "In June, 1987, I went to the Northwest territories again, this time to a settlement called Pond Inlet, just south of Griese Fiord. There were less than a thousand people there, and they had to bring in their oil for heating in the fall. They had to estimate it correctly well ahead of time, because, once it freezes up, it freezes solid. You can no longer bring ships in, and that's how they had to bring in the oil."

I said, "I always hear how expensive it is to live in Alaska... Now, why after you went to Griese Fiord, did you got to Pond Inlet? Wasn't it just more of the same? Or was it somehow different?"

Spies responded, "That's where I almost froze to death. That made it different."

We both laughed. I was learning to appreciate Dr. Spies' extremely dry sense of humor."

"Until I got sick, we photographed scenery mainly," Spies said. "There were very few animals.

"Our objective in going to Pond Inlet was to take a sled ride to the place where the water met the land. We were sure we would find lots of animals there to photograph. Because there was a storm, we changed our plans, travelling west, intending to go see a possible caribou herd. We didn't see any animals except for polar bears, but we did enjoy some beautiful scenery. We chased a mother polar bear and her two cubs a short distance, and I did get a few photographs of them.

"As I soon learned first-hand, you sink deep into the snow when you walk in it. You can't go very far before tiring. At one point, we saw the graves of two unfortunate people who were caught in the ice. I walked out to these graves to photograph them and quickly became exhausted."

Again, I was astounded by Dr. Spies' fortitude.

"We stayed out overnight on the ice, in tents. There were no toilet facilities anywhere, and it was men and women both." He chuckled. "We just had to go a short distance away from the camp and do what nature required."

I observed, "Sounds like pretty harsh conditions. And you were how old at this time?" I needed to confirm this.

"I was about eighty-five," he said. "Eighty-six, I guess. I didn't feel that at all. It's only in the last year and a half that I've had this trouble."

He was referring to his current heart condition that limited his physical activity.

"You mentioned earlier that you became hypothermic?"

"Oh yes," he said. "Those sleds...it looks like it's smooth riding. But it's a continual pounding, going over bumps. We travelled seventy-five to one hundred miles under these conditions. And I wasn't dressed properly. I was cold all the time."

"What were you wearing?" I asked. "That you weren't dressed properly?"

Spies smiled ruefully. "Well, I thought I was dressed properly, but I wasn't. My feet started getting cold. The way it affected me was that I lost my appetite. I didn't even want to drink water. I couldn't work my camera anymore because my hands were so stiff. And then I had these bruises on the back of my legs, big as saucers."

"From what?"

"From the pounding of the sleds," he answered. "And the only time I would get warm was in the sleeping bag at night. My heart was slowing down. I believe I was getting hypothermia, which, if it becomes irreversible, can kill you.

"There was a great big iceberg next to the place where we had camped on the ice. So the next day the tour guides moved the camp because they feared it might break off, and we'd be set out on the iceberg.

"However, rather than continue on with the tour, because of my illness from the cold, I made arrangements to go back with the woman who was on the trip."

"She was fed up too?" I asked.

"Oh no," he said. "She had planned all along to leave early and had already made plans to go back to civilization. No, she wasn't fed up. And I was sure that if I stayed there even one or two days more, it would be the end of me."

I nodded silently. It sounded as if he was right about that.

Spies continued, "When we went back, it was rather dangerous. We had all that distance to go, and there was was only one native guide and the woman and myself. The guide drove the snowmobile, and we rode in the sled back of that. And if anything would have happened on that long trip—" he shook his head "—why we would have been done for."

"If something had happened to the guide?"

"Right," he said.

I shook my head. "Boy, I don't think that's an adventure I would care to have."

"When I finally got home and got into my bed—in my nice warm bed—why I was really pleased." He chuckled.

"Then I hit the jackpot on the third trip to the Northwest territories, when I went to Hudson Bay and Churchill on Hudson Bay in the last part of October, 1987. I remember that trip quite well because I drove from Washington D.C. into Canada. I then took a small plane to Churchill, where I discovered a large number of polar bears to photograph. The bears were very photogenic. Churchill was actually the only place I went where I really got to take as many animal pictures as I wanted. Everywhere else I travelled, photographing animals was a bit of a disappointment.

"We travelled in a bus, so we were protected from the polar bears. They look harmless enough in some of my photographs, but they're really quite treacherous. We couldn't open the windows because they had been known to attack people through the open windows. Some polar bears came within ten or fifteen feet of us, an ideal distance for photography. I got a shot of one polar bear on his hind legs; he must have been six or seven feet tall.

"In Churchill the people take the polar bears very seriously. They provide shelters everywhere for people to duck into if they should see a bear. In fact, they have air raid sirens for this purpose. The siren alerts you so you can immediately go into a shelter.

"I also photographed arctic foxes and seals. The polar bears live on seals. The seals can stay under water for fifteen to twenty minutes at a time. When they come up for air, however, often polar bears are lurking nearby, ready to pull them right out of their holes.

"When we needed to relieve ourselves, we would go off into an area filled with shrubbery. One of the men on the tour checked it out first, to make sure there were no polar bears hiding in there. He carried a shotgun with him, not to shoot the bears, but to scare them away, if necessary.

"In 1989 I travelled south to Patagonia, to the southern five provinces of Argentina. This was down near the Antarctica, the southernmost tip of South America." He smiled. "I had gone from one extreme to another—first travelling to the northern most settlement in North America, now to the southern most settlement in South America."

It was truly amazing. One would think that the those trips up north—particularly that last hypothermic trip—would have satisfied that wanderlust.

Spies continued, "I flew out from New York, over the jungles of Brazil, on a nine-hour, non-stop trip to Rio de Janeiro, the former capitol of Brazil. We used a catamaran, which is two boats with a bridge connecting them."

"A catamaran?" I said. "What does it do different from other boats?"

He explained, "Well, unlike most boats, they can go right up to the edge of the land. I took a number of photographs at that time. We then took the Voyage of the Beagle, which is the voyage Darwin took when he made his first trip. Instead of going around Cape Horn, which is very stormy and a little farther south, he found a route north of there. It saved him from taking the riskier trip around the Horn.

"In Patagonia I photographed penguins, elephant seals, whales, and cormarants, a kind of sea bird. I was surprised to see that the penguins, even though they live near water, actually live in holes, just like badgers.

"Shortly before my trip to Australia, I passed out at home, falling unconscious on the floor in my basement. I had been ill recently and didn't realize that I'd gotten quite dehydrated. I put my foot on the bottom step to go upstairs, got dizzy, and passed out.

"It was probably not that serious—" he shrugged his shoulders "—although I was eighty-six years old at the time. I do remember feeling as if I were close to death. I was so relaxed when I regained consciousness that I didn't want to get up and struggle as I always had. But I did. Uppermost in my mind was getting ready to go to Australia."

By this time I could no longer be astonished. A spell like that—serious or not—would have stopped most octegerians from embarking on a trip. Not Dr. Spies!

Spies said, "I took a fourteen-hour trip directly from Los Angeles to Australia in late April, 1991. Unfortunately, in L.A., I had over twenty-four-hundred dollars worth of camera equipment stolen at United Airlines. And they would not do a thing about it. I could not get a cent from them. My home owners policy paid for it, and there was no reason that they should do that rather than United. I'll tell you—I'm sure that they stole it. I naively stored my equipment in a fancy aluminum case lined with protective rubber. I might just as well have put a sign on the camera equipment that said, 'STEAL ME.' The woman at the counter who took it in asked me all about the contents. I didn't know what she was asking those questions for. I soon found out.

"I had to replace part of that equipment on the trip, which, fortunately, I was able to do in Brisbane, Australia, using just my credit card and my passport.

"While I was in Australia, I photographed koala bears, kangaroos, wallabies, which are small-scale kangaroos, and killer crocodiles. The crocodiles are vicious. They'll eat—kill dogs and people."

I asked, "Were you nervous about photographing them?"

"Well, no, because we were in a boat. If the boat had sunk, we would have been nervous as hell." He chuckled. "I also had the opportunity to photograph the Great Barrier Reef, which extended for 1200 miles along the eastern coast of Australia. Because the boat had a glass bottom, I was able to take some terrific pictures of underwater fish and plants."

I said, "I believe you also photographed round rock formations?"

Spies nodded. "Oh yes. They were near Ayres Rock, which is very famous. It's right about in the center of Australia. And it's a rock that's about five miles going round, five miles in circumference. And reaches a height of two thousand feet. And there have been a number of people killed trying to climb Ayres Rock. And that's where we saw those round rock formations. They're sort of like the Badlands, but instead, they're rounded."

"Earlier, you mentioned something about an inexperienced pilot?"

Spies smiled. "Well, he looked like a young kid to me. And this was a small plane that we took from Ayres Rock back to the place that was our destination. It was after dark when we got in the plane. He took out a flashlight to see his instrument panel, which didn't increase our confidence very much." Spies chuckled, adding, "But we did make it all right.

"The trip to Australia lasted three weeks, which was almost too long. But we were treated very well.

"The next trip was to Alaska." He checked his notes. "We got on a ship with approximately seventy other passengers at Prince Rupert Island, taking the intercoastal route to Alaska.

"We finally ended up at Sitka, Alaska. I photographed glaciers, eagles, harbor seals, seagulls, killer whales, and humped-backed whales. I got some terrific photographs of a pack of fifteen to twenty killer whales circling in the water, preparing to feed on salmon."

I asked, "Did you get to know any of the other people who went on these trips?"

"As a matter of fact, I was always impressed by the people I met who went on these tours," Spies answered. "There were all different kinds of people, although many of them were scientists. I corresponded with a few of them for a short time."

We were finished talking about the trips Dr. Spies had taken. While we were chatting informally, he mentioned that he had donated a scholarship to a university.

Spies said, "I gave a scholarship to Tufts University, in the School of Veterinarian Medicine."

"Why do you have a scholarship at Tufts?"

"It's a long story," he said. "I was a member of the Thornton W. Burgess Society because he had had such an influence on me in my younger days. I got involved with them because they were trying to get a stamp with Thornton W. Burgess's picture. And Elvis got the stamp instead."

"Elvis over Thornton?" I asked. I couldn't help smiling.

Spies laughed, "Yes. It was a terrible disappointment at the time. I had even written a letter to the Postmaster General, describing the profound influence the Burgess stories had had in the development of my life-long love of animals—but it was all to no avail.

"Anyway, I became acquainted with a couple involved in trying to get the Burgess stamp passed, John and Georgia Flagg. John had an association with Tufts University and spoke of the school very highly. When I went to Tufts, I was impressed by the work that they do and the wildlife clinic they have there."

He chuckled. "On one of my trips to meet with John and Georgia Flagg, I stayed at a hotel. I decided to try out the bathtub— to sit down and have a bath and be luxurious about it. Well, I got stuck."

"Stuck in the tub?"

Spies nodded. "I couldn't get out no matter how hard I tried. I had resigned myself to staying in there all night. But then I remembered Archimedes. Do you know who he was?"

I struggled to recall. "He was a early Greek scientist?"

"Yes," Spies said, "a mathematician. I applied one of Archimedes' principles, in which he said a body is buoyed up by water. I filled the tub full of water and rolled right out."

We both laughed.

I commented, "That was quick thinking." I would have had to sit there until morning, waiting for the maid to discover me.

"Yes, it was." He smiled and continued, "Then I met Dr. Charles Sedgewick at Tufts. He is a veterinarian and is in charge of the Wildlife Clinic. If a deer is injured on the road, he'll go out and get it, bring it in, and try to save it. He is very well known and respected for his work there.

"As a matter of fact, they had an eagle named Bullet there, that they had rescued in Alaska. He had been shot and permanently injured by a bullet, hence, his name. When they got the bird, they took him to the Sitka Alaska Rehabilitation Center for medical care. Eventually, they brought him down to Tufts University, where he lived the rest of his life. He couldn't be released into the wild."

"Why is that?"

"Because he's injured," Spies answered.

"Oh, he's permanently injured."

Spies nodded. "Right. So they gave him to Tuft University, and he participates in demonstrations. And all that sort of thing."

Then Spies came back to his point. "I was so impressed by Tufts University and the work they do there that I provided them with a $50,000 endowment."

Joe Spies, Diane Davis and Bullet at the School of Veterinary Medicine, Wildlife Clinic at Tufts University.

"Now, what was the scholarship for, specifically?"

Spies explained, "It's an annual scholarship for a third- or fourth-year veterinary student—one who exhibits scholarly merit, is interested in wildlife medicine, and shows financial need.

"When I visited Tufts' Grafton campus in September of 1992, I exhibited some of my best photographs there. I also narrated a slide show of the various exotic animals I had encountered on my recent trips around the world, showing slides of everything from polar bears to penguins.

"I also gave a couple scholarships for $50,000 each to deserving undergraduate students in chemistry to the University of South Dakota. Recalling just how tough it was to go to school and cope with finances, I wanted to make it easier for future chemistry majors to focus on their educational objectives and not worry so much about how they were going to pay for tuition, let alone food or rent."

These generous donations were certainly noteworthy. They said something about Dr. Spies and his concern for future generations of chemists and veterinarians.

Spies added, "In 1991 I happened to see newsman Tom Brokaw's excellent exposé on the killing of defenseless animals for sport on NBC. I sent Mr. Brokaw a copy of my book *Big Cats and Other Animals: Their Beauty, Dignity and Survival*, noting in my letter to him that we are both USD graduates. He responded with a pleasant thank-you note, saying, 'It's always good to hear from USD graduates. We have an impressive roster of alums doing well.' "

14

Retired at Last

"After I stopped photographing animals," Spies said, "I started dreaming about them regularly. In one especially vivid dream, I was in a ghost town and a huge male lion was charging me. Just before he got to me, a little dog ran out in front of the lion. The lion attacked the dog and simply demolished him."

Dr. Spies and I were nearing the end of our interviewing process. Since Dr. Spies's doctors diagnosed him with a heart problem, he has had to restrict his activities. At age ninety he has now actually retired.

Dr. Spies' son Carl and Carl's wife, Karen, had been staying in Washington, D.C. for a while in a condominium, while their new house was being built in South Carolina.

Dr. Spies told me, "I tried to persuade him to stay, but he wouldn't go for it. I told him he could join the country club and learn how to play golf. He plays golf, but he doesn't know how." He chuckled.

"Do you play golf?" I inquired.

"Oh no," he said. "I could never hit that little ball. Jack Dempsey couldn't either."

It struck me later, on my last night in D.C., when Dr. Spies took me, Carl and Karen out to dinner at his favorite Chinese restaurant, how and why Dr. Spies was different from your typical Midwesterner—although I think he was still Midwestern right down to his toes, in spite of the sixty years spent in D.C.—he was a man who couldn't settle for standard Midwestern fare, meat and potatoes. He was a pioneer in both his attitude and his accomplishments.

I was a little surprised to hear Dr. Spies and his son avidly discussing happenings on "The Young and the Restless"—but I realized then that I was supposed to hear this. This was all part of Dr. Spies' experiment.

We resumed our interviewing process one last time.

I asked, Dr. Spies, "Do you have any regrets? Is there anything you would have done differently?"

Spies was silent for a minute, thinking over his answer. "One thing I would have done differently...I would have had more consideration of my wife, Renice. I tended to neglect her in pursuit of chemistry and photography. There are a number of things I could have done differently. Also, some of my girlfriends, I—I would have treated them more kindly.

"I think about those things I did that I regret, and—it's been somewhat painful. I wish that I'd behaved differently, but I guess we all have those things we can't undo."

Spies added, "When I was working in photography, going full blown on photography or scientific work, I didn't have time—I didn't think about these things because I didn't have time. I was preoccupied with what I was doing. But after I retired, I had more time to reflect on how I lived my life."

I observed, "It seems to me as if you're a very analytical person, and so the focus you took was on the scientific rather than emotional—"

He nodded. "Yeah."

"As far as your professional life goes, would you do anything different? I mean, if you had a whole other life to live?"

"No," Spies answered, shaking his head, "I couldn't have

done any different. I've far, far exceeded my earlier expectations. No, I don't have any regrets about that."

"So you wouldn't have decided, 'Nah, I'm not going into chemistry this time. I'm going to do something different.' "

He said, "I never wavered on that."

"You wouldn't have pursued photography full-time?"

"As a matter of fact, I went into photography because it was an outlet for my creativity. I would not like to be a photographer who had a studio and took portraits of people. That would bore me to death. Now, I like to make things like this." He held up a fantasy photo. "I get ideas and I work them out. That's the only thing that appeals to me in photography."

I asked, "It seems to me that the other type of photography you were talking about is more limited?"

"Well, it's sort of routine," he said. "You set your camera up, you know what exposure to have, you take the picture, you do the same thing with slight modifications for all of the people. Now that doesn't appeal to me at all.

"I don't have any regrets about going into chemistry or having photography as a hobby. Photography as I did it was an outlet for my creativity. It gave me a freedom that I didn't have in science. It presented a certain challenge, presented problems to be solved. It was not a 9-to-5 job. It was a 9-to the end of the problem, Saturday, Sunday, and holidays job."

"Did your work in chemistry suffer at all—because of your interest in photography?"

He shook his head emphatically. "Although my interest in photography seemed to rival my interest in scientific research, I always kept photography secondary to science until my retirement in 1973.

"You know—I've said this before—I received a strong set of values when I was in the Home. I learned how to work hard and that a person should work hard at a profession they love. I've said it before— 'it's amazing I get paid for this because I'd do it for free.' That's how strongly I felt about chemistry. There's a lot of drudgery involved, and you couldn't do the work unless you knew it was a means to an end. Life is much more interesting when you feel pleasure rather than just being a drudge. Of course, that's part of why I did photography too."

He added, "All of the prizes I won, publications of covers on magazines, and so forth, each one of those was an accomplishment that I prized very much."

I felt it was time to ask this question: "Dr. Spies, what do you most want to be remembered for?"

He thought carefully before answering. "My advocacy of animals. And my scientific work, of course. I have worked hard to be an animal advocate by photographing animals and writing about them— to increase interest in animals. My photography and my writings were my attempt to bring back a section of the world that gets a raw deal. Would that I could have done more."

His sincere regret made me pause for a moment. He had obviously done more than most people ever dream about doing.

I asked, "Dr. Spies, aside from your desire to help animals, what led you to do so much—to publish over eighty papers in the field of chemistry, to travel all over the world, to photograph animals, to exhibit, to publish animal books—why did you do all that, Dr. Spies, when most people would have been satisfied with accomplishing one-tenth of what you have done?"

Dr. Spies paused. He set his notes on the table, leaning back in his chair.

He said slowly, "Why have I done so much? I'll tell you. Hunger. Do you know what I mean by hunger? I started from nothing almost. And I became very hungry. Yes, that's what motivated me. My only means of satisfying that hunger was achievement.

"My method was to concentrate solely on one thing, to put everything I had into making something work. When I'd get done with that, there was always another goal." He laughed to himself.

"So you were pretty single-minded," I said.

Spies said, "Yes, I became that way."

That ended our interviews. I left Dr. Spies in Arlington, Virginia, getting on a plane that took me back to South Dakota to set down his story on paper.

I know now that the years in the orphanage created that hunger in Dr. Spies. And it was a hunger that never went away.

As I worked on the manuscript, I could feel that hunger, from all those miles away, motivating me to write, to help him tell his story the best way I could.

Endnotes

[1] Spies, J. R.; Bernton, H. S.; Stevens, H. "The Chemistry of Allergens. I. Isolation of an Active Fraction From Cottonseed." J. Allergy. 1939, 10 (2), 113-129.

[2] Spies, J.R. "Oilseed Allergens." Immunological Aspects of Foods. Catsimpoolas, N., Ed.; Avi: Westport, Conn., 1977; 317- 371.

[3] Spies, J.R. "Oilseed Allergens."

[4] Spies, J.R. "Oilseed Allergens."

[5] Spies, J.R. "Oilseed Allergens."

[6] Spies, J.R. "Oilseed Allergens."

[7] Spies, J. R. "Determination of Tryptophan in Proteins." Anal. Chem. 1967, 39, 1412-1416.

[8] He read briefly from this letter: "Dissatisfaction, in the early 1940s, in the use of existing methods for the determination of tryptophan prompted our studies. The first of our several papers on the subject was published in 1948 and the last in 1967. Originally we never intended to get so involved. We started out by simply trying to substitute sulfuric acid for the concentrated hydrochloric acid used in some existing methods to avoid the corrosive fumes of the latter acid. But, one thing led to another, so that this small beginning led to over four years of full-time research with the excellent technical assistance of Dorris Chambers part of this time.
"The experimental research was just plain pleasure. But

getting the results published was something else. Originally I attempted to publish the contents of this paper as four separate articles, little suspecting the grueling road that lay ahead. Three of these articles were submitted to the late Walter J. Murphy, editor of Analytical Chemistry, on May 10, 1948, and the fourth on October 6, 1948. A total of 135 pages of manuscript was thus being considered at one time. The reviewers were hard and in one case prejudiced to a point where I asked for and received his disqualification.

"During the ensuing months I answered the reviewers' many comments with a general statement and specific reply to each point raised. My responses totaled 62 pages overall with numerous revisions of the manuscripts. The final result was the combination of the four articles into one consisting of 71 pages of manuscript. Exactly one year to the day after the first submission, the revised manuscript was tentatively accepted for publication subject to more editorial revisions. The review process was onerous and a strong will was required to keep from giving it all up somewhere along the way. However, with one exception, I am deeply indebted to the anonymous reviewers who performed a difficult and seemingly thankless task "

He continued reading: "Although many other papers on the determination of tryptophan have appeared, especially in the last decade, our method filled a considerable need by many researchers following its publication in 1949, and indeed the original method and its subsequent modification still enjoys considerable usage."

[9] Abstract of the article "Milk Allergy":

"Milk allergy occurs primarily in infants and children under 2 years of age. It became more prevalent in the U.S. as breast feeding declined and feeding of cow's milk increased. Milk allergy (atopic and anaphylactic) has an immunological basis as distinguished from such diseases as lactose intolerance and galactosemia. The reported incidence of milk allergy varies widely from 30% in allergic children to 0.1 to 7% in nonallergic children. Symptoms of milk allergy are asthma, rhinitis, vomiting, abdominal pain, diarrhea, urticaria, and anaphylaxis. Crib deaths have been attributed to milk allergy. Prognosis is that milk allergy usually disappears by age 2. Milk proteins are the etiological agents in milk allergy. Milk contains from 12-14 immunologically distinguishable proteins, all of which are potential allergens. DPL [Diary Products Laboratory] is doing basic research on milk allergens to elucidate the mechanism of the allergic response to ingested milk. Demonstration of new antigens (potential allergens) generated by brief pepsin hydrolysis of four milk proteins-casein, a-lactalbumin, b-lactoglobulin and bovine serum albumin, is the basis for a new concept of the role of digestion products in immediate type milk and food allergy."

[10] Abstract for the paper "Allergens"
"The problem of isolation and characterization of allergens is complicated for many reasons, some of which are discussed. Included are: the present state of classificaton of allergens; the significance of the original elucidation of the polysaccharidic protein nature of the cottonseed and castor bean allergens in relation to isolation and chemistry of allergens in general; and the related concept that chemically different compounds may share common antigenic and allergenic determinants. Food allergy is especially complicated in that the products of digestion may trigger an allergic response. Based on demonstration of 12 new antigens generated by pepsin hydrolysis of milk proteins, we have suggested that the body immune system may be exposed to at least 100 new antigens, all of which are potential allergens, on ingestion of milk. Our results may explain why foods, in many cases, do not give a skin reaction on persons who give an immediate-type allergic responses on ingestion of the food."

[11] See note 8 above.

[12] The Central Maine Cat Club called the photographs "striking" and the text "neatly helpful." *The Washington Star*, which had published numerous photos of Dr. Spies by this time, said in their May 11, '58 book review section, "This book undoubtedly contains some of the best intimate feline studies ever made."

Cats Magazine, in the June '58 issue, called the photography in the book "outstanding" and said, "Dr. Spies has not been content just to pose his cats and to make 'pretty pictures.' Instead, he has taken the difficult road of also presenting them in such situations as, for example, their encounters with squirrels and birds; during courtship; in various forms of cat-calisthenics; and—in a rare technical and artistic triumph—with shining eyes in a tree-top at dusk."

The Christian Science Monitor, in the October 9, 1958 issue, called *Cats and How I Photograph Them* "a fine book for either shutterbug or ailurophile, and particularly for a person who is both"— an ailurophile, of course, being a lover of cats.

Publications

Scientific Publications (in chronologic order of publication)

Drake, N. L.; Spies, J. R. "Note: Mannitol from Haplophyton Cimicidum." *J. Am. Chem. Soc.* 1930, 52, 3739.

Drake, N. L.; Spies, J. R. "The Toxicity of Certain Plant Extracts to Goldfish." *J. Economic Entomology.* 1932, 25 (1), 129-133.

Spies, J. R.; Drake, N. L. "Two Constituents of Parosela Barbata (Oerst.) Rydb." *J. Am. Chem. Soc.* 1932, 54, 2935-2938.

Spies, J. R. "Improved Method of Sealing the Capillary Tubes in the Rast Modification of the Barger Method of Molecular Weight Determination." *J. Am. Chem. Soc.* 1933, 55, 250.

Spies, J. R. "The Toxicity of Certain Plant Extracts to Goldfish. II." *J. Economic Entomology.* 1933, 26 (1), 285-288.

Drake, N. L.; Spies, J. R. "A Simple Large-Capacity Extractor." *Ind. Eng. Chem.* (Analytical Edition). 1933, 5, 284.

Spies, J. R. "Croton Resin. I. Toxicity Studies Using Goldfish." *J. Am. Chem. Soc.* 1935, 57, 180-182.

Spies, J. R. "Croton Resin. II. The Toxic and Vesicant Action of Certain of its Derivatives." *J. Am. Chem. Soc.* 1935, 57, 182-184.

Drake, N. L.; Spies, J. R. "Croton Resin. III. The Combined Acids." *J. Am. Chem. Soc.* 1935, 57, 184-187.

Spies, J. R. "Recovery of Silver and Iodine from Silver Iodide." *Ind. Eng. Chem.* (Analytical Edition). 1935, 7, 118-119.

Spies, J. R.; Drake, N. L. "-Ribose from the Croton Bean" *J. Am. Chem. Soc.* 1935, 57, 774-775.

Spies, J. R. "Process for Obtaining Free Silver and Iodine From Silver Iodide." U.S. Patent 2 060 539, 1936.

Spies, J. R. "The Solubility of Nicotine Silicotungstate in Solutions of Dilute Hydrochloric Acid." *J. Am. Chem. Soc.* 1936, 58, 2386-2388.

Spies, J. R. "Determination of Small Quantities of Nicotine by a Silicotungstic Acid Micromethod." *Ind. Eng. Chem.* (Analytical Edition). 1937, 9, 46-47.

Spies, J. R. "Crotin Resin. IV. The Petroleum-Ether-Insoluble Acids." *J. Org. Chem.* 1937, 2 (1) 62-67.

Spies, J. R.; Harris, T. H. "Nitrogen Determination in Refractory Substances (By a Modification of the Dumas Micromethod)." *Ind. Eng. Chem.* (Analytical Edition), 1937, 9, 304-306.

Spies, J. R.; Bernton, H. S.; Stevens, H. "The Chemistry of Allergens. I. Isolation of an Active Fraction From Cottonseed." *J. Allergy*. 1939, 10 (2), 113-129.

Spies, J. R. "Isoguanine from the Crotin Bean." *J. Am. Chem. Soc.* 1939, 61, 350.

Spies, J. R.; Harris, T. H., Jr. "Some Salts of 2-Oxy-6, 8- diaminopurine." *J. Am. Chem. Soc.* 1939, 61, 351-352.

Bernton, H. S.; Spies, J. R.; Stevens, H. "Significance of Cottonseed Sensitiveness." *J. Allergy*. 1940, 11 (2), 138-146.

Spies, J. R.; Coulson, E. J.; Bernton, H. S.; Stevens, H. "The Chemistry of Allergens. II. Isolation and Properties of an Active Protein Component of Cottonseed." *J. Am. Chem. Soc.* 1940, 62, 1420-1423.

Spies, J. R.; Bernton, H. S.; Stevens, H. "The Chemistry of Allergens. III. The Solubility Behavior of an Active Protein Picrate from Cottonseed." *J. Am. Chem. Soc.* 1940, 62, 2793-2799.

Spies, J. R. "Recovery of the Cottonseed Allergenic Protein from its Picrate by Electrophoresis." *J. Am. Chem. Soc.* 1941, 63, 1166.

Spies, J. R.; Bernton, H. S.; Stevens, H. "The Chemistry of Allergens. IV. An Electrophoretic Fractionation of the Protein-Polysaccharide Fraction, CS-1A, from Cottonseed." *J. Am. Chem. Soc.* 1941, 63, 2163-2169.

Coulson, E. J.; Spies, J. R.; Stevens, H. "The Immunochemistry of Allergens. I. Anaphylactogenic Properties of a Proteic Component of Cottonseed." *J. Immunology*. 1941, 41 (4) 375-381.

Spies, J. R. "The Chemistry of Allergens. V. The Amino Acid Content of Active Protein and Polysaccharidic Protein Fractions from Cottonseed." *J. Am. Chem. Soc.* 1941, 63, 2994-2996.

Bernton, H. S.; Spies, J. R.; Stevens, H. "Evidence of the Multiplicity of Allergens and Reagins in Cottonseed Sensitiveness." *J. Allergy*. 1942, 13 (3), 289-295.

Spies, J. R.; Umberger, E. J. "The Chemistry of Allergens. VI. Chemical Composition and Properties of an Active Carbohydrate- free Protein from Cottonseed." *J. Am. Chem. Soc.* 1942, 64, 1889-1891.

Spies, J. R.; Chambers, D. C.; Bernton, H. S.; Stevens, H. "The Chemistry of Allergens. VII. The Nature of the Unidentified Allergens of Cottonseed." *J. Allergy*. 1942, 14 (1), 7-18.

Coulson, E. J.; Spies, J. R.; Stevens, H. "The Immunochemistry of Allergens. II. Antigenic Studies by the Dale Method of the Electrophoretic Fractionation Products of the Protein- Carbohydrate Fraction, CS-1A, from Cottonseed." *J. Immunology.* 1942, 46 (6), 347-365.

Coulson, E. J.; Spies, J. R. "The Immunochemistry of Allergens. III. Anaphylactogenic Potency of the Electrophoretic Fractionation Products of CS-1A from Cottonseed." *J. Immunology.* 1940, 46 (6), 367-376.

Coulson, E. J.; Spies, J. R. "The Immunochemistry of Allergens. IV. Effect of Dilute Acid on Anaphylactogenic Activity, Specificity, and Reagin-Neutralizaton Capacity of Cottonseed Allergenic Fractions." *J. Immunology.* 1943, 46 (6), 377-389.

Spies, J. R.; Coulson, E. J. "The Chemistry of Allergens. VIII. Isolation and Properties of an Active Protein-polysaccharidic Fraction, CB-1A, from Castor Beans." *J. Amer. Chem. Soc.* 1943, 65, 1720-1725.

Coulson, E. J.; Spies, J. R.; Stevens, H. "The Immunochemistry of Allergens. V. Comparison of the Rates of Dialysis of Crystalline Ovalbumin and of the Cottonseed Allergen, CS-1A." *J. Immunology.* 1943, 47 (6), 443-452.

Spies, J. R.; Coulson, E. J.; Chambers, D. C.; Bernton, H. S.; Stevens, H. "The Chemistry of Allergens. IX. Isolation and Properties of an Active, Carbohydrate-Free Protein from Castor Beans." *J. Amer. Chem. Soc.* 1944, 66, 748-753.

Coulson, E. J.; Spies, J. R.; Stevens, H. "The Immunochemistry of Allergens. VI. Anaphylactogenic Properties of a Proteic Component of Kapok Seed and the Relationship of Kapok-Seed Antigens to Cottonseed Antigens." *J. Immunology.* 1944, 49 (2), 99-116.

Spies, J. R.; Coulson, E. J.; Stevens, H. "The Chemistry of Allergens. X. Comparison of Chemical and Immunological Properites of CB-1A Preparations from Domestic Castor Beans and Brazilian Castor Bean Pomace." *J. Amer. Chem. Soc.* 1944, 66, 1798-1799.

Coulson, E. J.; Spies, J. R.; Stevens, H. "The Immunochemistry of Allergens. VII. A Study of the Homogeneity of Cottonseed- Globulin Preparations by Anaphylactic Reactions." *J. Allergy.* 1945, 16 (4), 176-183.

Spies, J. R.; Chambers, D.C.; Bernton, H. S.; Stevens, H. "Quantitative Estimation of the Absorption of an Ingested Allergen." *J. Allergy.* 1945, 16 (6), 267-274.

Coulson, E. J.; Spies, J. R.; Jansen, E. F.; Stevens, H. "The Immunochemistry of Allergens. VIII. Precipitin Formation and Passive Transfer Reactions with Allergenic Proteins from Cottonseed and Castor Beans." *J. Immunology.* 1946, 52 (3), 259-266.

Spies, J. R. "3. Recovery of Silver and Iodine from Silver Iodide Residues." *Inorg. Syntheses* II 1946, 49 (2), 6-9.

Spies, J. R.; Chambers, D. C. "Chemical Determination of Tryptophan." *Anal. Chem.* 1948, 20 , 30-39.

Spies, J. R.; Chambers, D. C. "Photochemistry of Tryptophan, p-Dimethylaminobenzaldehyde and Reaction Products in Sulfuric Acid Solution." *J. Amer. Chem. Soc.* 1948, 70 , 1682-1685.

Spies, J. R. "Some Derivatives of L-Tryptophan." *J. Amer. Chem. Soc.* 1948, 70, 3717-3719.

Coulson, E. J.;Spies, J. R.; Stevens, H. "The Immunochemistry of Allergens. IX. The Relationship of Carbohydrate to the Antigenic Properties of the Allergenic Protein from Cottonseed." *J. Immunology*. 1949, 62 (2), 171-182.

Spies, J. R.; Chambers, D. C. "Chemical Determination of Tryptophan in Proteins." *Anal. Chem.* 1949, 21, 1249-1266.

Spies, J. R. "Dimorphism of Formyl-D- and L-Methionine and the Effect of Hydrochloric Acid on the Rotation of D- and L- Methionine." *J. Biol. Chem.* 1950, 182 (1), 439-443.

Coulson, E. J.; Spies, J. R.; Stevens, H.; Shimp, J. H. "The Immunochemistry of Allergens. X. Anaphylactogenic Properties of Allergenic Fractions From Castor Bean." *J. Allergy*. 1950, 21 (1), 34-44.

Spies, J. R.; Chambers, D.C. "Utilization of Optical Isomers ofMethionine and Formylmethionine by Some Lactobacilli." *J. Biol. Chem.* 1950, 183 (2), 709-712.

Spies, J. R.; Chambers, D. C. "Determination of Tryptophan with p-Dimethylaminobenzaldehyde Using Photochemical Development of Color." *Anal. Chem.* 1950, 22, 1209-1210.

Spies, J. R. "Determination of Tryptophan with p- Dimethylaminobenzaldehyde." *Anal. Chem.* 1950, 22, 1447-1449.

Coulson, E. J.; Spies, J. R.; Stevens, H. "Identification of Castor Bean Allergen in Green Coffee." *J. Allergy*. 1950, 21 (6), 554-558.

Spies, J. R. "Oilseed Allergens." *Treatment of Asthma*. Abramson, H.A., Ed.; Williams & Wilkens: Baltimore, 1951; Chapter 14; 271-276.

Spies, J. R.; Chambers, D. C. "Spectrophotometric Analysis of Amino Acids and Peptides with Their Copper Salts." *J. Biol. Chem.* 1951, 191 (2), 787-797.

Spies, J. R.; Coulson, E. J.; Chambers, D. C.; Bernton, H. S.; Stevens, H.; Shimp, J. H. "The Chemistry of Allergens. XI. Properties and Composition of Natural Proteoses Isolated from Oilseeds and Nuts by the CS-1A Procedure." *J. Amer. Chem. Soc.* 1951, 73 3995-4001.

Spies, J. R. "An Ultraviolet Spectrophotometric Micromethod for Studying Protein Hydrolysis." *J. Biol. Chem.* 1952, 195 (1), 65-74.

Spies, J. R.; Chambers, D. C.; Coulson, E. J.; Bernton, H. S.; Stevens, H. "The Chemistry of Allergens. XII. Proteolysis of the Cottonseed Allergen." *J. Allergy.* 1953, 24 (6), 483-491.

Spies, J. R. "Colorimetric Procedures for Amino Acids." *Methods in Enzymology III.* Colowick, S.P.; Kaplan, N.O., Eds.; Academic Press: New York, 1957; 467-477.

Spies, J. R.; Chambers, D. C.; Coulson, E. J. "The Chemistry of Allergens. XIII. Ion-Exchange Fractionation of the Cottonseed Allergen and Immunological Properties of the Products." *Arch. Biochem. Biophys.* 1959, 84 (2), 286-296.

Spies, J. R.; Bernton, H. S.; Chambers, D. C. "Quantitative Analysis of Allergens by a Passive Transfer Method as Demonstrated with Fractions of Cottonseed Allergen, CS-1A." *J. Allergy.* 1960, 31 (2), 162-174.

Spies, J. R.; Bernton, H. S.; Chambers, D. C. "Quantitative Measurement of the Migration of Intracutaneously Injected Cottonseed Allergen in Passive Transfer Studies." *J. Allergy.* 1960, 31 (2), 175-180.

Spies, J. R.; Coulson, E. J.; Bernton, H. S.; Stevens, H.; Strauss, A. A. "The Chemistry of Allergens. XIV. Effect of Heat and pH on the Precipitin Reaction and Reagin Neutralizing Capacity of the Castor Bean Allergen, CB-1C." *Annals of Allergy.* 1960, 18, 393-400.

Coulson, E. J.; Spies, J. R.; Stevens, H. "The Allergen Content of Castor Beans and Castor Pomace." *J. Amer. Oil Chem. Soc.* 1960, 37 (12), 657-661.

Spies, J. R.; Bernton, H. S. "Response of Nonallergic Persons to Injected Castor Bean Allergen, CB-1A." *J. Allergy.* 1962, 33 (1), 73-83.

Spies, J. R.; Coulson, E. J.; Bernton, H. S.; Well, P.A.; Stevens, H. "Castor Bean Components: The Chemistry of Allergens. Inactivation of the Castor Bean Allergens and Ricin by Heating with Aqueous Calcium Hydroxide." *Agricul. and Food Chem.* 1962, 10 (2), 140-145.

Spies, J. R.; Coulson, E. J.; Wells, P. A. "Deallergenization and Detoxification of Castor Bean Pomace" U.S. Patent 3 101 266, 1963.

Spies, J. R.; Coulson, E. J. "The Chemistry of Allergens. XVI. Ion Exchange Fractionation of the Castor Bean Allergen, CB-1A, and Antigenic Specificity Relationships of the Fractions." *J. Biol. Chem.* 1964, 239 (6), 1818-1827.

Morris, R. S.; Spies, J. R.; Coulson, E. J. "The Chemistry of Allergens. XVII. Disc Electrophoresis and Gel Diffusion of the Carbohydrate-Free Allergenic Protein, CB-65A, from Castor Beans." Arch. Biochem. Biophys. 1965, 110, 300-302.

Spies, J. R.; Coulson, E. J. "Antigenic Specificity Relatonships of Castor Bean Meal, Pollen, and Allergenic Fraction, CB-1A, of Ricinus Communis." J. Allergy. 1965, 36 (5), 423-432.

Spies, J. R.; Barron, J. K. "The Chemistry of Allergens. XVIII. An Analysis of CB-1A From Castor Beans." Annals of Allergy. 1966, 24, 499-502.

Spies, J. R. "The Chemistry of Allergens. XIX. On the Number of Antigens and the Homogeneity of the Isolated Antigens of Fraction CB-1A From Castor Beans." Annals of Allergy. 1967, 25, 29-34.

Spies, J. R. "Determination of Tryptophan in Proteins." Anal. Chem. 1967, 39, 1412-1416.

Spies, J. R. "Determination of Tryptophan in Corn (Zea mays)." Agricul. and Food Chem. 1968, 16 (3), 514-516.

Spies, J. R. "New Antigens Generated by Brief Pepsin Hydrolysis." Internat. Dairy Congress. 1970, 1E, 50.

Spies, J. R.; Stevan, M. A.; Stein, W. J.; Coulson, E. J. "The Chemistry of Allergens. XX. New Antigens Generated by Pepsin Hydrolysis of Bovine Milk Proteins." J. Allergy. 1970, 45 (4), 208-219.

Spies, J. R. "New Antigens in Lactose." Proc. Soc. Exp. Biol. and Med. 1971, 137 (1), 211-214.

Spies, J. R.; Stevan, M. A.; Stein, W. J. "The Chemistry of Allergens. XXI. Eight New Antigens Generated by Successive Pepsin Hydrolyses of Bovine B-lactoglobulin." J. Allergy and Clin. Immunology. 1972, 50 (2), 82-91.

Spies, J. R.; Stevan, M. A.; Stein, W. J. "A Method for Estimation of the Relative Antigenic Potencies of Preparations Containing Common New Antigens Derived From a Precursor Protein (B-Lactoglobulin)." J. Immunological Methods. 1972, 35-43.

Spies, J. R. "Milk Allergy." J. Milk and Food Technology. 1973, 36 (4), 225-231.

Spies, J. R. "Allergens." Agricul. and Food Chem. 1974, 22 (1), 30-32.

Spies, J. R.; Stevan, M. A.; Stein, W. J.; Gordon, W. G. "The Chemistry of Allergens. XXII. Isolation and Characterization of Three New Antigens from the Dialysates of Six Successive Pepsin Hydrolyses of B-Lactoglobulin." Int. Arch. of Allergy and Applied Immun. 1975, 48, 49-71.

Spies, J. R. "Oilseed Allergens." *Immunological Aspects of Foods.* Catsimpoolas, N., Ed.; Avi: Westport, Conn., 1977; 317- 371.

Non-Scientific Publications

Big Cats and Other Animals: —Their Beauty, Dignity and Survival. Hollywood, Florida: Frederick Fell Publishers, 1988.

The Compleat Cat: The Private Life of the Cat From Kittenhood to Courtship. Revised edition. Englewood Cliffs, New Jersey: Prentice-Hall, 1984.

Il Mio Amico Gatto. Italy: Calderini, October, 1983 [Italian version of *The Compleat Cat*].

Wild Ponies of Chincoteague. Cambridge, Maryland: Tidewater Publishers, 1977.

The Compleat Cat: The Private Life of the Cat From Kittenhood to Courtship. With Prize-winning photographs. New York: Bonanza Books (Prentice-Hall), 1966.

Cats—and How I Photograph Them. New York: The Studio Publications, 1958.

Awards and Recognitions

Scientific Awards/Special Recognition

Elected to Phi Beta Kappa at the University of South Dakota, 1926.

Elected to Sigma Xi at the University of Maryland, 1931.

Co-winner of the Hillebrand Prize in 1950, along with H. Stevens and E. J. Coulson, for work on the chemistry and immunochemistry of allergens at the USDA. The Hillebrand Prize is awarded annually for original contributions to the science of chemistry by a member or members of the Chemical Society of Washington.

President of the American Chemical Society of Washington, 1958.

Certificate presented in recognition of fifty years of membership in the American Chemical Society. January 1, 1983.

Non-Scientific Awards/Special Recognition

Received the University of South Dakota Alumni Association Alumni Achievement Award. Vermillion, South Dakota. 1971.

Heritage Club, University of South Dakota. Membership conferred "in recognition of Your Generosity." 1981.

Received an Honorary Doctor of Humane Letters degree from the University of South Dakota. 58thSummer Commencement, Vermillion, South Dakota.
August 6, 1987.

Scientific/Professional Memberships

Alpha Chi Sigma.
The Allergy Society of Greater Washington
The American Academy of Allergy
The American Association for the Advancement of Science
The American Chemical Society.
The American Society of Biological Chemists.
The American Academy of Allergy.
The American Association for the Advancement of Science.
The Cosmos Club.

The Society for Experimental Biology and Medicine.
Phi Beta Kappa.
Sigma Xi.
The Washington Academy of Science

Non-Scientific Memberships

The Animal Welfare League of Arlington. Arlington, Virginia.
The Thornton W. Burgess Society.

Radio Talk Show Interviews—1990

March 15. WBVT (4:05 p.m.) Pittsburgh, Pennsylvania.
March 17. KSTR (10:00 a.m.) Grand Junction, Colorado.
March 19. American Radio Network (10:05 a.m.) Baltimore, Maryland.
March 22. WLAL (3:00 p.m.) Nashville, Tennessee.
March 23. WMOX (2:00 p.m.) Meridian, Mississippi.
March 28. WBCK (1:35 p.m.) Battle Creek, Michigan.
April 2. Dr. Michael Arnoff (11:00 a.m.) White Plains, New York.
April 4. WHP (3:10 p.m.) Harrisburg, Pennsylvania.
April 10. KNST (3:20 p.m.) Tucson, Arizona.
April 17. WHND (9:30 a.m.) Monroe, Michigan.
April 17. WOAI (5:00 a.m.) San Antonio, Texas.
April 27. KTAR (3:00 a.m.) Phoenix, Arizona.
April 30. WMDO (7:00 p.m.) Wheaton, Maryland.

Scholarships/Endowments

Established an endowment with the University of South Dakota Foundation to be used for chemistry scholarships. Vermillion, South Dakota, 1986.

Establish a $50,000 endowment with Tufts University to be used for an annual scholarship for a third- or fourth-year veterinary student.

The Animal Welfare League of Arlington. Arlington, Virginia. Donated copies of Cats and How I Photograph Them as prizes for donations of $100 or more.

The Humane Society. Donated 47 photos of cats for their publication, *Shelter Sense*. 1988.

The National Zoofari Silent Auction for the Washington National Zoological Park. Donated signed books and zoo animal photographs to help raise money for completing Amazonia, the Zoo's new tropical rainforest exhibit and education center. 1990

Photographic Art of Joseph R. Spies

Atlas Lion

Cicadacide
Capital Chemist, March 1956

Cats, Cats, Cats

Bookworm

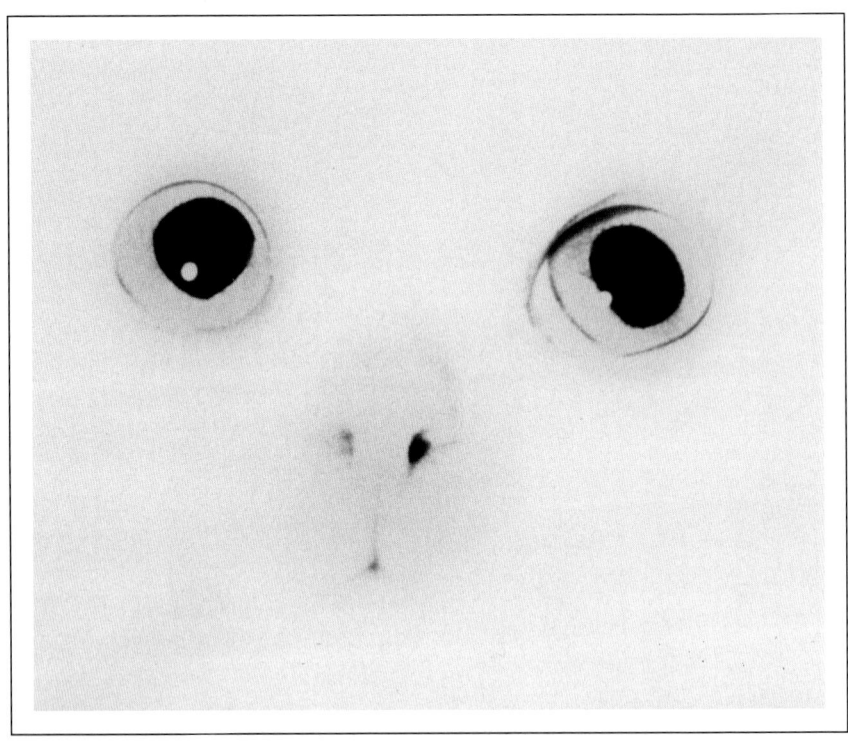

White Cat
Popular Photography Contest Prize Winner, 1956

Black Cat.
Night Flying

Bakers Dozen
Washington Star, 1954

Merry Christmas
Cover, Capital Chemist, 1958

Peek-a-boo

Contact

The End is Near
The Washington Star, 1957

Photomontage
Attack
Counterattack
Surrender

Washington Post, 1963
National Observer, 1963
Scholastic Magazine, 1964

Granddaughter Lauren Spies with Tiggar

Complete Trust

Time to Get Up
The Washington Star, 1952

The Chess Player
Calendar

Pepper
The Washington Star, 1952

Magazine, 1968

How Do You Do?
The Washington Star, 1954

...ut to Lose Face

Cover
Cats Magazine, 1960

Cover
Cats Magazine, 1971

Meal-time Handicap.
Cats Magazine, 1966

Acrobatic Cat

Untitled
The Capital Chemist, 1957

Big Cats and Other Animals

White Tiger

Leopard

Bald Eagle

Wild Ponies of Chincoteague

Timber Wolves

Timber Wolf

Gorilla

White Tiger and Cub

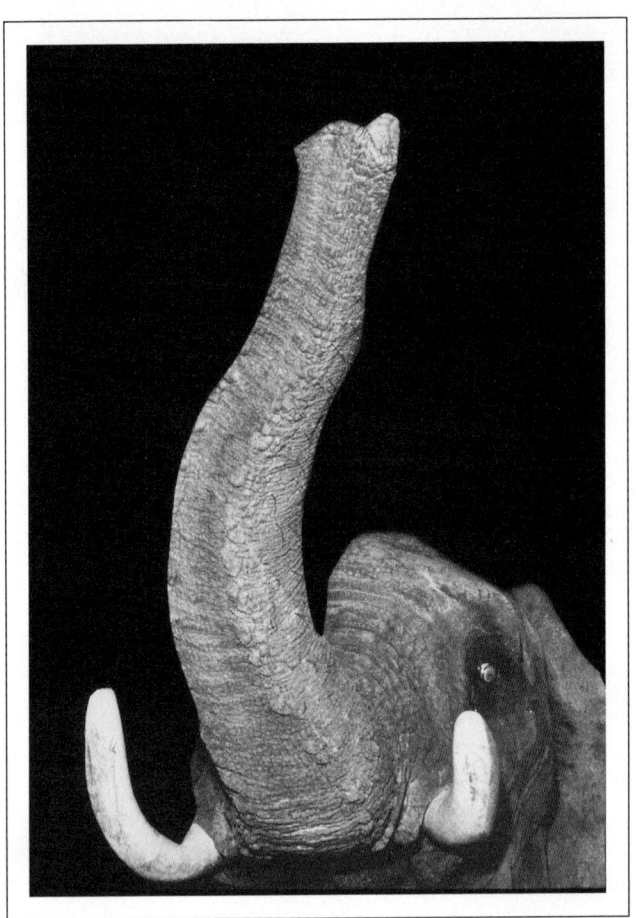

African Elephant

Snowy Owl

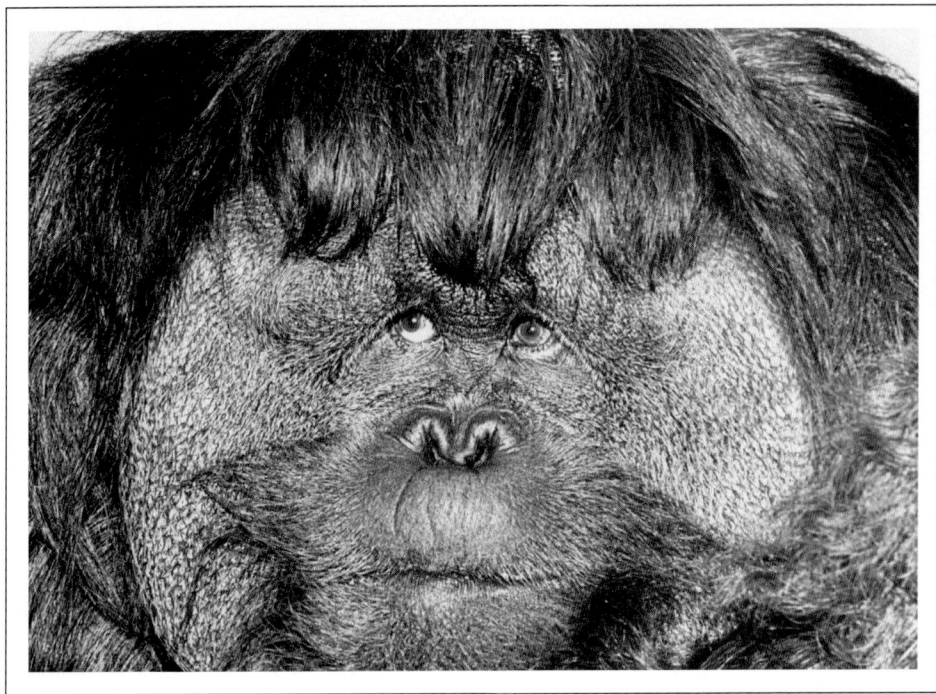

Orangutan

Asian Elephant

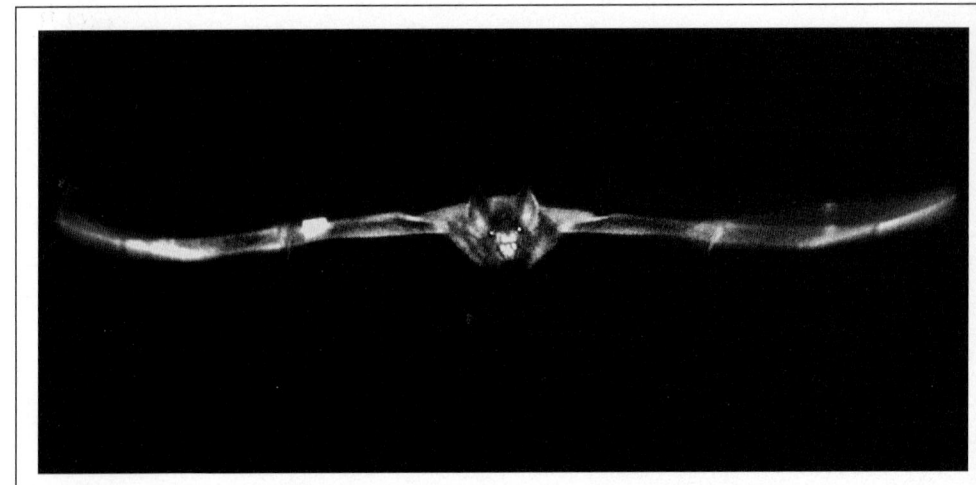
Short-tailed, Leaf-nosed Bat

Egyptian Spiny Mice

Brown Wood Owl

Frogmouth Owl

Kodiak Bear

yenas

Tiger by the Tail

Female Lion

Cheetah

Atlas Lion

Hippopotamus and Baby

rus Cranes

Cheetah

Jaguar

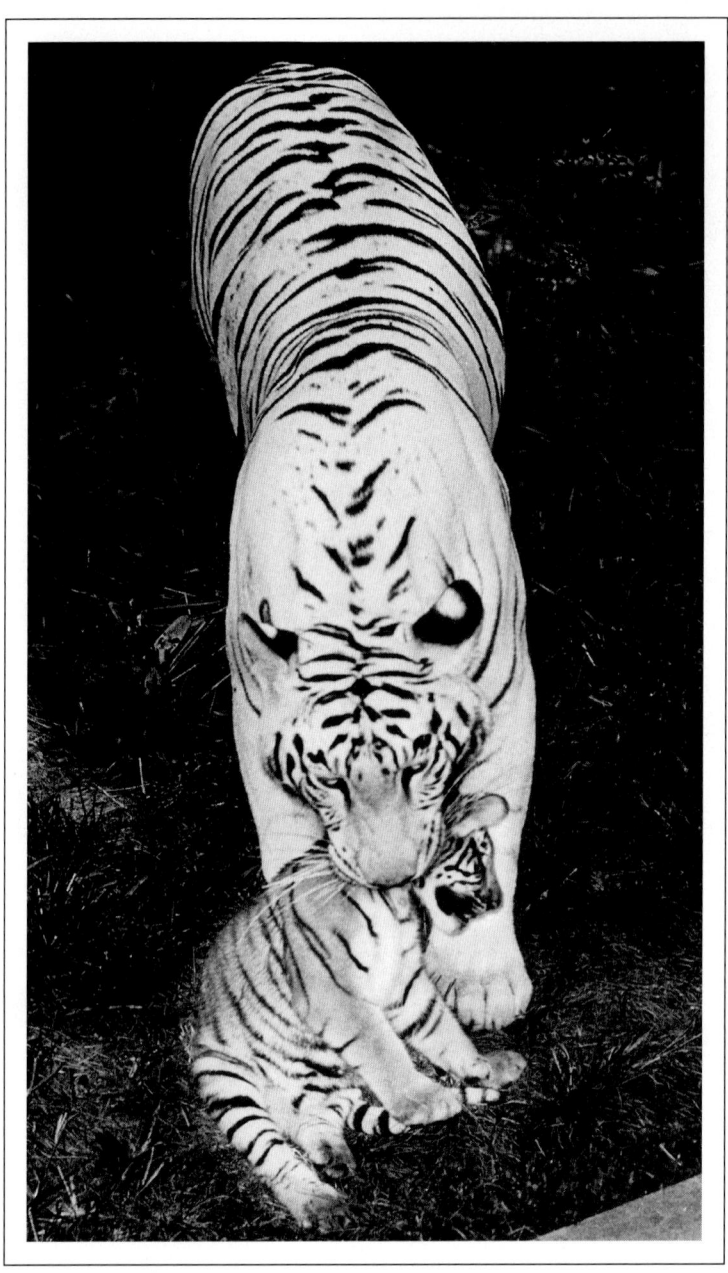

White Tiger and Cub

Ouch!

En Garde

Touche

Tough Guy

Tiger

Cat Fantasies

Wild Flight of Fantasy

Cleanup

The Hills Have Eyes I

The Hills Have Eyes II

Sunset Watch

Doomsday

Looking for the Pot of Catnip at the End of the Rainbow

Halloween

Birds---Squirrels---and Other Living Things

Surprise!
Washington Star and Daily News Prize Winner, 1972
Back Cover, World, *National Geographic,*
National Enquirer, *1978*

Blue Jay Dive Bomber

Peanuts Flying

Parakeets Not Welcome Here

Eating Peanuts

Opossum and Racoons

Two Blue Jays
Washington Star Prize winner, 1972
Eastman Kodak International Contest Special Merit Award
Photographing America, *by Eastman Kodak*

Squirrels Fighting Over Peanuts

Three Blue Jays

Two Blue Jays Fussing Over Peanuts

Two Blue Jays Flying Over Peanut Bowl

King of the North

Arctic Scene